D1014029

THE DEFENSE NEVER RESTS

A Lawyer's Quest for the Gospel

CRAIG A. PARTON

CONCORDIA PUBLISHING HOUSE • SAINT LOUIS

To Professor Rod Rosenbladt
For first teaching me that all Scripture is about Christ (John 5:39)
and then pointing me to a church that practiced it.
Your defense of Christ our Advocate has never rested.

Copyright © 2003 by Concordia Publishing House
3558 S. Jefferson Avenue, St. Louis, MO 63118-3968
Manufactured in the United States of America

Library of Congress Cataloging-in-Publication Data

Parton, Craig A., 1955–
  The defense never rests : a lawyer's quest for the Gospel/ Craig A. Parton.
    p. cm.
    ISBN 0-7586-0482-3
  1. Lutheran Church—Doctrines. 2. Evangelicalism—Lutheran Church. 3. Lutheran Church—Liturgy. 4. Evangelicalism and liturgical churches. I. Title.
BX8065.3.P37 2003
230′.41—dc21   2002155735

1 2 3 4 5 6 7 8 9 10   12 11 10 09 08 07 06 05 04 03

CONTENTS

FOREWORD

It has been said that since the books most borrowed from public libraries deal with Abraham Lincoln, with doctors, and with dogs, a surefire literary hit would be a book titled *Lincoln's Doctor's Dog*. We doubt it very much, but Craig Parton's book is unique in that it does successfully speak to three diverse audiences, all of whom badly need the message he delivers with such logic and panache.

The first of these audiences is Evangelicalism. Parton recognizes its strength: an active, dynamic presentation of the "simple Gospel" of salvation through Christ's shed blood. That message saved the author—and, in remarkably parallel fashion, the writer of this foreword. When I was an undergraduate at Cornell University, representatives of Inter-Varsity Christian Fellowship (a slightly more intellectual Campus Crusade) dragged me kicking and screaming into the Kingdom by showing me the bankruptcy of Protestant liberalism and my need for a Savior from sin.

But, like Parton, I was not long in discovering the lack of depth in Evangelicalism. I, too, found my way to Lutheranism—by comparing the doctrinal positions of Lutheranism, Calvinism, Arminianism, and Roman Catholicism against the teachings of the Greek New Testament. Lutheran theology came out ahead at every point—and I, with no liturgical background whatsoever, found myself stumbling through the Common Service and loving every minute of it.

Parton rightly shows the Evangelical the way to a theology far more powerful than anything the television evangelists have ever offered. And he helps them to see that the theological options are not limited (as virtually all Evangelicals believe) to Calvinism, Arminian Methodism, and Dispensationalism. Parton rightly argues that Lutheran theology and churchmanship would provide today's Evangelical with exactly what he needs: a thoroughly biblical, genuinely Christ-centered theology drawing upon the spiritual resources of the entire history of Christendom.

Second, Parton speaks to the Lutherans themselves—who, as Garrison Keillor has so well shown, often function as "God's frozen people." Delighted with *"Gottes Wort und Luthers Lehre,"* the orthodox Lutheran often leaves evangelism to the Evangelicals and refuses (in spite of holding to the inerrancy of Scripture) to obey the Petrine command to "be prepared to give an answer [Greek, *apologia*] to everyone who asks you to give the reason for the hope that you have" (1 Peter 3:15). The favorite excuse is that to present facts such as evidence for the resurrection of Christ in support of the faith is to go against "salvation by grace through faith." Parton decisively refutes such nonsense. If God chooses to reveal Himself in this world, as He most certainly has, then the presentation of the evidence for that incarnation is precisely in accord with the Gospel. If Parton's solid apologetic were to be taught and practiced the length and breadth of Lutheranism, we would see far more informed faith commitments. Faith is not credulity; it is based on fact and is meaningless without a solid foundation in fact. Lutherans do not have "faith in faith"; they have faith in a God who was factually "reconciling the world to Himself in Christ" (2 Corinthians 5:19).

Third, in this book Parton speaks to the religious liberal and to the secularist. As a lawyer, schooled in rigorous standards of evidence, he shows that Christian faith—while speaking to the deepest needs of every person—is not a matter of emotion and subjectivity, but an issue of truth for which there is a better case than there is for contrary viewpoints. To the religious liberal he says: would the kind of poor reasoning your historical-critical method represents hold up for one minute in a responsible court of law? To the uncommitted he says: you are the jury; can you bring in any verdict other than the vindication of the Christian Gospel and Scripture in light of the evidence in their behalf?

It is always gratifying to read and recommend the work of a former student—especially when that student has become a colleague. Craig Parton not only carries on a prestigious trial practice in the oldest law firm in Santa Barbara, California, but also serves as American director of my International Academy of Apologetics, Evangelism, and Human Rights, held in Strasbourg, France, each summer (www.trinitysem.edu). There he has shown his effectiveness in training believers to defend the faith once delivered to the saints. Now his fascinating book—autobiographical, theological, and apologetical—will carry that message to a wider audience of those who very definitely need to hear what he has to say.

PROF. DR. JOHN WARWICK MONTGOMERY

Introduction
Whatever Happened to the Gospel?

In the past 20 years a number of prominent Evangelical churches have stopped displaying the cross in their sanctuaries. Bill Hybels, pastor of a leading American mega- (and crossless) church in Illinois, observed that pagans are offended by the cross. Some fast-growing churches have discovered that the world likes Jesus the Moralist and Jesus the Conservative Family Values Man. As for Jesus the atoning Lamb who died for the sins of the world, who suffered our deserved fate on that cursed tree, and who was indeed wounded for our transgressions—well, He just isn't selling seats like He used to. The real Jesus apparently has a serious marketing problem. Dr. D. James Kennedy of the renowned Coral Ridge Presbyterian Church recently sent out a massive mailing of gold crosses with a corpus attached thereon. So? Only one problem— upon the cross hung the corpus of the American flag. Self-proclaimed Christian teachers chastise those who use non-seeker friendly biblical terms like *damnation, wrath, hell, torture, rebellion, sin, blood, cross, death, grace, mercy, redemption, substitution, justification,* and *salvation.* And such was I—in fact, chief among them.

After many years as a zealous Evangelical and full-time missionary, I realized how little actual preaching of the pure Gospel I was engaging in and how little confidence I had in the power of God's Word to crush human pride and to create saving faith. My confidence in my self-created "means of grace" was limitless— there were few groups I couldn't persuade by adding a frothy chaser of biblical morality, the latest principles of communication, and the tried-and-true appeal to "felt needs." The last thing on my mind after becoming a Christian in 1974 was ending up in the Lutheran (aka "dead") church. Lutherans, in my view, needed conversion. They didn't *have* the Gospel—they *needed* the Gospel.

My journey out of generic American Evangelicalism is not especially remarkable. Witness the recent exodus of Frankie Schaeffer to Eastern Orthodoxy (along with scores of former Campus Crusade for Christ staff members almost two decades ago). Witness Thomas Howard, Scott Hahn, and Peter Kreeft's journeys to Roman Catholicism as well as Robert Webber's move to Episcopalianism. Witness Michael Horton and the throng that has exited to Calvinism. No, an exodus from Evangelicalism is not remarkable. What is odd is that I landed where escapees do not generally flock to—the conservative Lutheran Reformation.

At the pure stream of the Lutheran Reformation, I found the Gospel *at the center* once again—not just a polite mention of it. I found a Christ willing to save even me, a sinful and failing Christian. For the first time I found the Scripture taught with Christ in His saving office at the center of the sermon, with confidence that the authoritative Word was able to shatter hearts of stone and calm the terrified conscience of the guilty sinner.

I found a church where my children were instructed to get on their knees and confess their sins rather than shout, clap, and giggle. I found the artistic tradition of Albrecht Dürer and Lucas Cranach, the musical genius of J. S. Bach and Felix Mendelssohn, and a love for the natural world found in Johann Kepler and Tycho Brahe.[1] The arts were affirmed as great gifts for use in worship because they placard Christ and the Gospel. I finally found reverence and a

God I could again fear as well as love and trust. I found a link to the historic and universal (i.e., catholic) worship of the church. I found a church where one didn't simply ask if Mrs. Smith or Elder Jones likes the music, but whether it was a song that Abraham, Moses, and the apostles and prophets—better known as the communion of the saints—would gladly sing because of its solid doctrine and similarly substantial melodic line. I found an earthiness in Luther and the Lutheran Reformation that was refreshing—a freedom in the Christian life I did not think possible without becoming theologically liberal.

But, most important, I found Christ crucified as the center and substance of Lutheran worship. I found a doctrine of the Christian life that flowed out of the forgiveness of sins and that let God do the saving and the sanctifying from start to finish. In short, I found the Gospel for me as a Christian. I found what it really meant to be evangelical.[2] The journey was, and continues to be, difficult for me and my family. More than ever, I believe that Lutheranism's connection to the ancient church can make it appear unfriendly to the modern-day Evangelical. Our journey to Lutheranism has resulted in the loss of friends and vibrant, large youth groups. My children have seen their parents choose churches—and then leave churches—solely for reasons of doctrine. I fear for the countless Evangelicals who are ready to dump the church altogether rather than continue in a thinly veneered Sunday-morning version of the consumer-driven, info-byte secularism they live in all week. The "holy trinity" of newness (i.e., be hip), numbers (i.e., be big), and needs (i.e., be relevant) now provides the dominant "means of grace" within much of Evangelicalism.

In Lutheranism I indeed found the evangel—the Good News —as the focus of its prayed, spoken, and sung confession. Yes, I found some things I thought were foreign additions—vestments, altars, candles, pipe organs, corporate confession of sin, kneeling benches, old hymns, written prayers, and a "liturgy" (whatever that was) conducted according to an equally unheard of "church year."

But I also found Christ at the center of all of it and the reason for all of it.

I am a trial lawyer by profession. The best trial lawyers identify the central issue critical to the success or failure of a case. A successful trial lawyer can take the most complex case and distill it to its essence. When one asks the various branches of the Christian faith what is at the center and heart of their theology, one gets a surprisingly wide variety of answers. For Rome, the sacrifice of the Mass is that upon which the church rises or falls. For Constantinople and Eastern Orthodoxy, the sublime mystery of the Holy Trinity and man's privilege to partake of the divine is central. In Calvin's Geneva, the sovereign election and workings of God in eternity are the starting points. Thus, Rome speaks of a life lived in and from the sacraments. Orthodoxy speaks of a life lived in prayer, mystery, and contemplation.[3] Calvin speaks of a life lived under the sovereignty of God and the enlightenment and joy that come from following the Law and serving God and others.[4] Luther, however, speaks of the life of the Christian as centered *sub crucis*—"under the cross."

Lutheranism gets the cross right—why it was necessary, what it accomplished, how I am saved, and how that salvation is delivered to me as still a wretched sinner today. Lutheran theology, teaching, and worship anchor the life of the redeemed believer in Christ and His cross.

Thus, this is *not* the story of leaving Evangelicalism. It is the story of realizing what was missing and then finding authentic evangelicalism in the evangel of Jesus Christ.

1

THE GOSPEL IN FOUR LAWS
A GOLD BOOKLET FOR BLACK PAGANS

I was a garden-variety pagan when I went off to California Poly-technic University in 1973. My father had died suddenly that past February from a brain tumor. My 18 years up to that point had been lived in Christian Science.[1]

My first step out of Christian Science occurred on February 12, 1973, around noon in the waiting room of St. Francis Hospital in San Jose when my father's brain surgeon met us outside of the operating room. His eyes averted downward—not a good sign. He took my mother, my brother, and me to the hospital chapel and told us there was nothing else he could have done for my father. He was dead. During the operation, he said, my dad had needed more than eight pints of blood. The doctor's surgical apron gave evidence of the complications. It was splattered with my father's blood—irrefutable confirmation that matter was real. The implications were startling—might sin, death, and the devil be real also? I went to college adrift in reluctant unbelief.

My bags were hardly unpacked in the freshman dormitory when members of Inter-Varsity Christian Fellowship descended upon me and immediately and aggressively preached the evangel to me—Christ died for sinners and I qualified. These people would not be denied. My questions were met with reasoned responses. My unbelief was shown to be conceived and maintained in ignorance. Old Adam, however, would not be easily silenced. I spent the summer after my freshman year working for a liberal congressman in Washington, D.C., embroiled in debates against pro-lifers and Christian fanatics who believed that my employer was demonic. The proverbial "Hound of Heaven," however, was on my trail.

One Evangelical group in particular attached themselves to my fleeing backside in the fall of 1974 and would not release. Staff members of Campus Crusade for Christ simply would not let me rest in unbelief. They presented a gold booklet to me called "The Four Spiritual Laws." These "laws" were as follows: (1) God loved me and had a wonderful plan for my life; (2) I had sinned and fallen short of the glory of God; (3) I could not save myself by my good works and was on the way to a deserved hell; and (4) I must receive Jesus Christ as my Lord and Savior.

Thus I heard the Gospel once again, this time in 1974. I believed. I later was informed that by an act of my will I had decided to receive Christ. John 1:12 was the proof text. Salvation was a free gift and totally undeserved (Ephesians 2:8–9), but an act of my will threw the regeneration process into gear. But almost as soon as I was ushered into salvation's front door, a second message with an equally compelling voice reverberated from every corner. I was told that the gold booklet had a different function for me now that I had made the decision it had demanded. The purpose of that booklet was now to share it with others. As a Christian believer I was to move on to mastering a blue booklet entitled "How to Live the Spirit-Filled Life." Something more was needed beyond the gold booklet—I needed to live an obedient life, and the blue booklet had the answer. Thankfully, I thought, at least I can exercise my free will in this decision, too, and can throw the process into gear. Of course, my free will had to keep on making right decisions under the terms of the new booklet. The gold booklet had asked for one, and only one, decision in the past.

The blue booklet (called the "birdie booklet" by Campus Crusade staff because of the picture of the dove on the cover symbolizing the Holy Spirit) was my introduction to Evangelicalism's central doctrine—practical Christian living, sanctification, or the all-critical "how-tos" of the Christian life.[2] Practical living, sanctification, how-tos—it all added up to the same thing. Letting God work in my life was a daily election in which I held the deciding vote. God was for me and the devil against me. I could break the tie with an act of my will. There were various tested methods to assist me in casting the correct vote that accomplished the all-critical disciplining of my sinful flesh. These methods would prepare the way for the Spirit's unseen but all-important work in my heart. So it was vital that one memorize verses, pray, join a fellowship group, read the Bible, fast, avoid key sins, go to conferences, and witness.

During my senior year I was involved with an even more intense group than Campus Crusade—a kind of modern-day evangelical monastic movement called The Navigators Christian Fellowship. I committed entire books of the Bible to memory (a good thing, no doubt, in principle). However, I soon experienced a "spiritual hierarchy" within Navigators based on Bible verses memorized, length and location of prayer and "quiet times" (tops of mountains were favored), and the number and location of conferences attended (e.g., distance traveled from California for a conference was an indication of commitment). The Navigators encouraged spiritual disciplines that came along with book titles such as Oswald Chambers's *My Utmost for His Highest*. (Years later I remembered this approach to the Christian life when reading of Luther's days as a monk and the well-developed and eminently practical monastic system that created and sustained the so-called medieval "ladders of ascent" used to cooperate with the grace of Christ in order to live at the highest levels of spirituality.[3] A truly committed life was the goal and heaven was on the line. The pursuit of the ladders of ascent led Luther to the brink of insanity. He concluded that he really hated the God who required what so obviously could not be performed.)

The danger sign that I did not perceive at that time and that was much too subtle to detect was this: The Gospel of Christ's saving work for sinners (i.e., the forgiveness of sins or the doctrine of justification, which Luther calls the doctrine on which the church stands or falls) was not the focus or the source of "power" for the daily life of the repentant and forgiven Christian. I needed help in practical Christian living. I needed "how-tos." If I knew better, was the assumption, I would do better. More conference notebooks filled with exhortations to godly living began to fill my shelves. Surely, I reasoned, God would not demand things of me in the Bible if I had no power to fulfill what He demanded.

LIFE LIVED IN EVANGELICALISM: FROM LAW TO GOSPEL TO LAW

The Gospel had definitely been there to get me, by a decision of the free will, *into* the Kingdom. It was, by definition, for *unbelievers*. What Christ accomplished by living a sinless life, by going to the cross to suffer and die, and by being resurrected from the dead was to be preached to unbelievers. But now I was a Christian. Some hinted at the fact that we were still sinners, but the important conference podiums and pulpits of the megachurches I attended were filled by advocates of victorious, sanctified, and practical Christian living.

Here is what I was taught: God the Holy Spirit had been handed the baton by God the Son. God the Son did the critical work in the past for sinners in dying on the cross and, more important, was resurrected and was now permanently in heaven listening to our prayers. Thus, the empty cross was an appropriate icon in the Evangelical churches I attended in those decades. Christ wasn't here anymore—He was in heaven reigning victoriously. Reigning victoriously was also what I was supposed to be doing. The Holy

Spirit, however, was in this world and works now. God the Father had high expectations for me that could all be accomplished through obedient cooperation with the Holy Spirit. A sanctified "higher life" (through what Campus Crusade called the practice of "spiritual breathing") was awaiting me if I would learn to "yield." By my decision to receive Christ I got the engine started on a cold January morning. But the car was pretty well stuck in the garage until a second decision to walk in the Spirit each moment of each day threw the car into gear. The hope was that the gear would be drive. My personal experience showed me to be more often in reverse or at best in neutral.

My Baptism two years after my conversion reflected the continual focus within Evangelical circles on my life. Prior to my immersion, the pastor of my nondenominational Bible church asked for my "testimony." I recounted a decent tale of a wayward life and my conversion. Much of the story involved the practical changes in my life since conversion and evidences of those changes being "real." My story of course had the advantage of involvement with a cult. My testimony reflected what was central to me and the audience—a changed life. Rather than pointing to Christ as John the Baptizer did, I pointed to my response to Christ. A seemingly innocuous distinction? It is, in fact, a distinction with a lethal difference. Why? Because my response to Christ simply was not (and is not) the Gospel!

A rhythm to what I was being taught was developing. As an unbeliever I had heard about my sin and my need for a Savior. As soon as I believed the Gospel, however, I quickly heard the list of jobs for me to do around the house. This rhythm of directing me immediately back to works after hearing the Gospel and the forgiveness of sins (i.e., a rhythm of Law-Gospel-Law) was my daily diet received from Evangelicalism's best pulpits and conference centers. Ironically, I later learned that this is the same rhythm found in Roman Catholic theology. It is, therefore, unsurprising that many Evangelicals are converting to Rome. The rhythm of Law-Gospel-

Law was not understood by me as doctrinal confusion at the time. The theological categories of Law and Gospel and the biblical roles of each either do not exist or are not taken seriously outside of the Reformation. Such theological clarity does not exist in Evangelicalism and cannot unless there is a return to the Reformation.

I experienced what happens when Law and Gospel are not understood and thus not distinguished. My Christian life, truly begun in grace, was now being "perfected" on the treadmill of the Law. My pastors did not end their sermons by demanding that I recite the rosary or visit Lourdes that week in order to unleash God's power; instead, I was told to yield more, pray more, care about unbelievers more, read the Bible more, get involved with the church more, and love my wife and kids more. Not until I came to the Lutheran Reformation some 20 years later, did I understand that my Christian life had come to center around my life, my obedience, my yielding, my Bible verse memorization, my prayers, my zeal, my witnessing, and my sermon application. I had advanced beyond the need to hear the cross preached to me anymore. Of course, we all knew Jesus had died for our sins, and none of us would ever argue that we were trying to "merit" salvation. But something had changed. God was a Father all right, but a painfully demanding one. I was supposed to show that I had cleaned up my life and was at least grateful for all the gifts that had been bestowed.

What had my Evangelical training done to me? The Gospel was critical for me at the beginning, critical to now share with others, and still critical to get me to heaven, but it was of little other value. The "evangel" in Evangelicalism was missing. My Evangelical training had me on a treadmill of merit. My "solid Bible training" was killing me.

2

THE GRANDEUR
OF AMERICAN EVANGELICALISM

My training in Evangelicalism had given me certain founda-
tional commitments. The grandeur of American Evangelicalism rests in its zeal for the lost and in its conviction that people
without Christ are truly condemned to an eternity of getting what
they deserve—namely a hell where the fire is not put out and the
worm does not cease to gnaw. People need Christ and need to be
converted. With this evangelistic zeal comes the highest regard for
Scripture as the inerrant Word of God. Evangelicalism taught me
that the Scripture is without error and is to be taken in its natural
and often disturbingly literal sense. This literalism had particular
application whenever the subject turned to the beginning of time
(Genesis and creation) or the end of time (Revelation and eschatology), which was almost every Sunday. Elaborate banners were
strung out across the church stage on many Sundays that set out
with a remarkable degree of precision the timing of either the creation or Jesus' return. But when, for example, end-times events did
not turn out to be as exact and "prophetic" as anticipated (e.g., the
European Common Market was not the Antichrist, Desert Storm
did not foretell Armageddon, Henry Kissinger was not the Great

Harlot of Revelation), the teacher or author simply let the ground lie fallow for awhile. I was regularly involved with churches that centered their interests on the beginning or the end of time. These topics are ones in which American Evangelicals can engage in their chief recreational activity—speculation.

Evangelicalism also taught me an aversion to theological Liberalism and works righteousness (aka Roman Catholicism)—the kind displayed by Rev. Eccles in John Updike's novel *Rabbit Run* or reflected in the limp-wristed minister in the film *Simon Birch*. Catholics were clearly presumed unsaved—guilty till proven innocent. In similar need of salvation were all whose confidence in salvation rested in a reliance on their Baptism as infants. This included Lutherans whom I found to be largely incapable of defending their position. The Eastern Orthodox might as well be from the planet Melmak—I had never met nor heard of such a position and would have surely lumped them together with Catholics if I had met one since vestments + incense + icons = Rome = unsaved, in my Evangelical calculus. I did meet some Evangelicals who had discovered the writings of John Calvin and had promptly ceased doing evangelism based on their understanding of Calvin's doctrine of election and the sovereignty of God.

Evangelicalism also stood tall in its emphasis on a theology that criticized the structures of society. It stood against social quietism. The Scripture had made an impact on society in the areas of law, politics, the family, and human rights. Abortion, homosexual rights, banning of prayer in school, euthanasia, and the legalization of pornography were issues that Evangelicals fought *against*. Sermons on these themes were part of my regular diet. On the other hand, positive contributions by Evangelical Christians to culture in areas such as non-pop music, film, poetry, art, and literature were hard to find and still are. Evangelicalism in general either naively accepts culture or reacts against culture; it is not well equipped to contribute to the culture. The best that can be hoped for is that Amy

Grant becomes so popular that she can sing songs with ambiguous lyrics that unbelievers like.

Finally, I gained a deep respect for the apologetical task from Evangelicalism. The questions of unbelief were treated seriously. Evangelicals were prepared for questions the unbeliever had. Evangelicals did not wait for pagans to wander up and ask, "How then shall I be saved?" They actively went out and engaged the culture. I remain deeply impressed with, and indebted to, this aspect of Evangelicalism.

DONNING THE PITH HELMET: JOINING CAMPUS CRUSADE FOR CHRIST STAFF

My undergraduate years found me dabbling in the ever-propagating para-church Evangelical groups. I spent time in Campus Crusade, Inter-Varsity Christian Fellowship, and The Navigators. In fact, I met my wife through involvement with The Navs. But throughout my undergraduate years I was only marginally involved in Campus Crusade. I never attended a Crusade conference during undergraduate days. I was a most unlikely candidate for full-time Christian ministry. My goals were entirely academic—to obtain strong grades and to go to law school. By the end of my senior year I had applied to and been accepted to law school. Events then took a different turn.

In March of my senior year I was approached by Campus Crusade staff about my future. Had I considered full-time campus work with Crusade? Why not? Shouldn't I at least pray about coming on staff and see what God wanted? I prayed. Within weeks I was on my way to Campus Crusade national staff training in Colorado. I raised all of my financial support from unbelieving friends and family. To their credit, Campus Crusade sent me to a place where I could do the least harm—a land where coyotes outnumber people—The University of Wyoming in Laramie.

In Wyoming I joined the other staff people for Campus Crusade in the state—all three of them. The fields were white unto harvest. Whatever I wanted to do I could. I commenced preaching the Gospel in fraternities, sororities, and classrooms. I participated actively in my local Evangelical church (Wesleyan Methodist) and made lasting friendships with the pastor and his family who were—and are—"evangelical" in the very best sense.

Three years later, in 1980, Campus Crusade provided the opportunity for me to travel and speak on university campuses across the United States in an effort to bring the Gospel to college students. I visited more than 75 campuses, speaking in countless fraternities, sororities, classrooms, free-speech settings, debates, and weekend retreats. I preached and taught in scores of Evangelical churches of all denominations across the country (except Lutheran, Catholic, or Eastern Orthodox—from which no invitations were forthcoming and to which none of our students or staff to my knowledge ever went). I was growing increasingly uneasy, however, with the content of my talks. All too often the "hook" to get in to speak to groups was a "felt-need" topic that required a contrived transition to anything remotely resembling a Pauline presentation of the Gospel of Christ crucified for sinners.

My interest in apologetics was growing, as is to be expected when you are dealing with unbelievers in the university context. My need pushed me to read serious theology and apologetics. C. S. Lewis, G. K. Chesterton, Dorothy Sayers, and John Warwick Montgomery became favorites. They linked the Christian faith with the noblest expressions of western intellectual and artistic culture and presented it as eminently reasonable and defensible. My debates on campuses exposed the tender underbelly of my learning. For the most part, I was not reading primary sources. More often, I was reading people who had read those who had read the primary sources. I was engaged in a very dangerous enterprise—speaking to the very limits of my knowledge.

In 1982 I was given the opportunity one February evening to meet Dr. John Warwick Montgomery, who at that time had earned a mere seven advanced degrees. He now has ten—his latest is a Master of Laws, with a specialty in canon law. Through his books *History and Christianity* and *Christianity for the Tough-Minded,* as well as his debates with the likes of Thomas J. J. Altizer, Bishop Pike, Madeline Murray O'Hare, and Joseph Fletcher, I had come to view him from afar with the deepest respect. Montgomery was lecturing at a secular college in California on "Legal Evidences and the Case for the Resurrection of Jesus Christ." I attended and was overwhelmed with the breath of his learning and the Christocentric nature of his apologetical presentation. Christ crucified was the center of the lecture. It was of the highest scholarly content and in no sense demeaning to the searching unbeliever. Most important, no effort was made to remove the offense of the cross or to "sell" Christianity based on the higher lifestyle it offered. Montgomery's trial-lawyer focus and clarity (he is an American attorney and English barrister) astounded me. Shortly thereafter I began academic work under Montgomery, Dr. Rod Rosenbladt, and Dr. Walter Martin at the Simon Greenleaf School of Law, where I received the degree of Master of Arts in Christian Apologetics in 1984.

At Simon Greenleaf I received my first real education. The course on "Classical and Contemporary Theology" was a comparison of Rome, John Wesley, and the Reformation on the critical doctrines of Scripture (i.e., God, man, sin, Christ, Holy Spirit, the church, end times). Rosenbladt was the professor. The class was my introduction to the historic efforts in the Christian church to systematize the teachings of Scripture around the central doctrines. It was in Rosenbladt's class in 1983 that I first heard of the disturbing similarities in the doctrine of the Christian life between Rome and Evangelicalism as seen in Wesley. For both Rome and Wesley the doctrine of sanctification had swallowed up the doctrine of justification. By way of contrast I was introduced to the theology of the Reformation through extensive reading in Luther and Calvin.

Though they were both "Missouri Synod" Lutherans (whatever that meant), neither Montgomery nor Rosenbladt ever pushed a church address on me. Quite the opposite. Names on church doors meant very little to them—the "smell" test was what that church in fact believed, taught, and confessed. At Simon Greenleaf I was trained to defend C. S. Lewis's *Mere Christianity*. Any push to convert to Lutheranism was not a topic—ever. Rosenblatt simply taught the theological distinctions within the branches of Christendom. It was here that I first heard an explanation of why chaos occurs in theology when the distinction between Law and Gospel is blurred in the pulpit. It was here that I discovered for myself Luther's Christocentric focus and the "conserving" nature of the Lutheran Reformation, as opposed to the radical reformation of the Swiss reformer Zwingli and the resulting effort to reduce the worship service to that which can be found specifically sanctioned in the Bible.

The road I was on at that time is only now clear to me. From an interest in evangelism I had been led to studying apologetics and the defense of the Christian faith through the ages. My reading led me to study church history and the historic efforts to clarify and systematize Christian doctrine. Professors Montgomery, Rosenblatt, and Martin pushed me to learn from the giants in the faith who had dealt with the key objections to Christianity first raised centuries earlier and at a time that the objections were often most clearly and persuasively stated.

Even more disquieting was that my interest in evangelism had not just led me to an interest in apologetics. It led me to an interest in the legal defense of the biblical Gospel—legal apologetics. The legal defense of the Gospel was leading me to look seriously at the law as a profession that provided direct tie-ins to the Gospel. Montgomery had directed me in this fascinating study of why lawyers had been historically attracted to the Christian faith and how legal standards of evidence could be employed in defending the Christ who was crucified under Pontius Pilate.[1] By the time I had presented my master's thesis on the nineteenth-century Anglican apologist Archbishop Richard Whately in a public defense at Simon Greenleaf in

1984,[2] I was already accepted to the University of California, Hastings College of the Law for the fall term of 1984. Three years later I had my Juris Doctorate and was headed to the firm of Price, Postel, and Parma in Santa Barbara as an associate attorney in the litigation and trial department.

From an interest in evangelism to an interest in apologetics to an interest in the law. I was on a path. What was it I was seeking to defend as a legally trained Christian apologist? Why, the Gospel of course. But where was the clearest doctrinal expression of the Gospel? Was there a theology that centered on getting the Gospel straight and putting that at the center?

The quest for clarity and for a Christ at the center was now leading me to an intellectual conclusion—Lutheranism was thoroughly Christocentric and clear. More disturbing, it was not "liberal" (though it is so perceived sometimes because many "Lutherans" of all stripes are simply Lutheran in name only and are unaware of, or indifferent to, the faith) and definitely not Roman Catholic either. They had some peculiar views on Baptism and the Lord's Supper, it seemed to me, because they were too literal with the biblical passages. This was a troubling realization. In addition, the overwhelmingly consistent testimony of church history on the topics of Baptism and the Lord's Supper was on Lutheranism's side. I also had the uncomfortable feeling that what my Evangelical teachers said Lutherans believed was not consistent with what the Lutherans actually believed—for example concerning what was going on with these earthly elements when combined with God's Word. It was not a work being offered up to God. Furthermore, just because the minister wore a robe and had people kneel up at an altar did not mean he was trying to hide his liberalism and latent works-righteousness. No, they were saying it was Good News—God coming *to me* and confirming and delivering *to me* the forgiveness of sins won at the cross. The recipient was meriting nothing. Perhaps kneeling was not a uniquely Roman Catholic liturgical body position.

Despite a gradual theological and intellectual reformation, my wife and I remained in nondenominational Evangelicalism for almost a decade longer. Why? The social and cultural ties were strong—we understood and genuinely liked these people. The church service was not always terrible or at least not regularly embarrassing. It was not great—but generally not bizarre either except at holidays or inevitably when guests were invited (e.g., Christmas pageants, cute-children-on-the-stage Sunday school programs, and "Purgatory Sunday," aka the Fourth of July). All of our friends were converts to Christianity with "born again" experiences. They were enthusiastic about reaching others and serious about mission outreach and studying the Scripture—though with more of an emphasis on Law than Gospel. Skipping Bible study class was not an option for us or our Evangelical friends. I regularly taught apologetics to classes overflowing with eager learners. Almost everyone in the church was seemingly involved in some kind of "ministry," loosely defined as using your talents for Christ.

However, the worship service often lacked reverence. That much was clear. During the week in the courtroom I dressed in my best clothes to show respect to the court. I stood when the judge entered. I rose and kept silence when the court spoke. Dignity, decorum, honor, order—all were part of my daily work life. I lived the "legal liturgy" six days a week. But Sunday was different. Why was it, I wondered, when in the presence of God we had yuppies in shorts and sandals acting like sophomores in high school?[3] Could I seriously invite professional (or any?) friends to a show with cheesy piano-bar-type music and giggles? And where in the congregation were the people near death—those old and infirm saints who had no "glowing life" to share but only the aches, pains, loneliness, and fears of nearing the end of this earthly existence?

One never really knew when our Sunday service started. Music just kind of moved into a welcome, which moved into announcements, which moved into "special music" (i.e., "music" by a person or persons with a microphone). One Communion Sunday I witnessed two young men in front of my family playing with the Communion wafers with their tongues and laughing. The worship service followed the "God is a very cool dude" theology of my congregation. The songs had God right there with me, hurting with all my hurts. But all the while I was coming to a terrifying conclusion: I had lost respect for the God who would welcome this sort of drivel. My wife and I—for the first time in 20 years of being ardent Evangelicals—began making excuses to our children for missing Sunday worship.

A SACRAMENTAL CRISIS

I found that I could put up with an enormous amount of nonsense in Evangelicalism. Then we had children.

I had, up to that time, endured teary-eyed testimonials; flag-waving July Fourth church services; pastors who worked the aisles like a talk-show host; Sunday school classes that consisted of the leader asking, "What do *you* think this verse means?"; special music featuring mother-daughter duets on Father's Day; and a boatload of pro-family values sermons and other assorted exhortations to moral living. Again, more Law than Gospel. But the beginning of our recognition of a need to hear Christ crucified from the pulpit again began with a crisis over the place of water, bread, and wine in the Christian life.

From my first days as an Evangelical I learned that Baptism was *our* act of obedience. The Lord's Supper was a memorial of what went on that somber Thursday night. We were taught that wine was not a good idea since grape juice was more likely used (reasoning that our Lord would not condone strong drink on such a solemn occasion, and we mustn't tempt alcoholics, never mind the fact that grape juice as a pasteurized, unfermented beverage was unknown until the nineteenth century.[4] More important, since this was only a memorial and symbolic act, the actual elements used were flexible. What was in your heart was more important than what you put in your mouth. Of central importance was the obedience you showed when reenacting these "ordinances." The flow of these acts was from earth to heaven—"sacrificial."

To replace infant Baptism, we had "baby dedications." After our first such experience in 1987, I vowed never to do that again in the event God ever forgave me and allowed us to have a second child. The "dedication" was all about my wife and me and what we would do to obey God and raise the child up. The direction was again clearly from earth to heaven. We vowed to be promise keepers. But promises by sinners, who are promise breakers by nature, to be faithful parents is not a recipe for comfort. Comfort comes from assurance that all is in our Lord Jesus Christ's hands and secure in His promises.

The same theology we found behind Baptism held true for Communion. God was not doing something for me in Communion (i.e., speaking and delivering the forgiveness of sins that Christ earned on the cross more than 2,000 years ago). To the contrary, I was doing something to show my love and commitment to God.

My wife and I had, of course, not baptized our children as infants. That would have been a works-oriented Roman Catholic rite since we were taught that an infant surely can't have faith and only faith saves.[5] But the day did come for my children to be baptized. They met with the pastor, who was reasonably assured that they had a testimony of a personal encounter with Jesus and being born again. One Sunday evening as I stood in the shadows to the side of the baptismal Jacuzzi, I watched my children address a sea of questioning faces and give their testimony. My children have since told me it was one of the most distressing days of their lives, since they constantly wondered if the audience believed their stories. They wondered if they even believed their own stories.

This event once again had a rhythm to it—a focus or direction. And once again that direction was from earth to heaven. We showed by our story that we had a changed life and were now expressing obedience by being baptized. God was the recipient and observer of all that was done. Confidence was based on our story and reciting a date and time when *we* had done something.

We were on a train that was heading for a crash. My wife and I were already struggling with the Lutheran Reformation's view of what was going on in the Lord's Supper. I was making the critical mistake of actually reading Luther and Martin Chemnitz, and they were hoisting me on my own Evangelical petard by arguing that the Words of Institution given by our Lord on that night before He was betrayed were best understood in their natural and therefore literal sense.[6] If Lutherans were wrong about this "real presence" of Christ in the Lord's Supper, their error was in taking the words too literally. In short, I was rapidly concluding that if Lutheranism was wrong, the apparent result was a higher view of the Lord's Supper than I presently maintained. In a worse case, I would be thinking I received more than I actually did receive. Calvinism's view of the Supper was not entirely comprehensible to me nor comforting in that the communicant could be two places at once (at the altar feeding on the elements and in heaven feeding spiritually on Christ who is chained to the right hand of the Father) and yet Christ could only be in one place (namely heaven).

Then that fateful Sunday came in the midst of this struggle, where Communion was to be administered. Of course, grape juice was used. That bothered me. Couldn't we at least take that part of Scripture literally? This was especially irksome since we were on our 135th week of sermons on the Book of Daniel, in which we were given all kinds of literal interpretations of seemingly obscure and figurative statements. We were instructed to not partake of Communion unless we had "clean hearts." Well then, I thought, the only honest people in this church are those who do not partake, since no one can know the depth of his sin. My children grabbed the "crackers and juice" (the terms used by the pastor) as they passed their way. I don't recall if Christ's Words of Institution were read.

But it was what happened after that service that provided the knockout punch. I lost site of my children. When I discovered them, one was gobbling the Communion "crackers" left carelessly in the foyer by the ushers. Her response when confronted by my utterly aghast expression was perfectly logical—"But I was hungry." Of course. She had been instructed from the pulpit—this was "crackers and juice" time and she was hungry. Just like snack time in third grade.

That was our last Sunday. We were desperate—desperate enough to try a church where we would not be surprised every Sunday. I called Dr. Rosenbladt in Los Angeles. I needed a face-to-face meeting. Now. After hearing my story and seeing my desperation, he encouraged me to go to a Lutheran church in Santa Barbara. His parting words rocked me: "First, whatever you do, do not choose a church based on their youth group. And second, when you do visit, listen to what they say about Christ." The two best pieces of advice I've ever heard on what to look for and what not to look for in a church.

It was Holy Week. The service we attended was on a Friday evening. It was called the "Service of Tenebrae." We were not prepared for what we found.

3

THE JOY OF REDISCOVERING SIN

G ood Friday 1995 began like any other Good Friday. Utterly
uneventful. The Evangelical church calendar I lived under did
not mark this day as anything but another day to "praise the Lord."
An Evangelical friend of mine, however, invited me to a "service"
at noon at the sunken garden in front of our courthouse in Santa
Barbara. Considering that desperation was pushing me to take my
family that evening to a Lutheran church, I figured I would give
Evangelicalism one last chance at the plate to bring me into contact with the Gospel, with the church ancient and, if I was really
lucky, with transcendence and mystery.

A GOOD FRIDAY WORSHIP SERVICE
OF FRIVOLITY

This particular noon service was set outside among palm trees,
freshly painted white stucco walls, and the Spanish-style architecture
of our magnificent courthouse. A stage was placed prominently in
the middle. Eager, smiling, happy people warmly greeted everyone.

I was first struck by the music—upbeat, soft rock done by a
James Taylor wanna-be backup band. Wireless microphones were
attached to the lapels of performers acting as if they were doing a

"gig" for Jesus. Everyone was laughing, smiling, joking—it was all very cute and fun. The testimonials and the message sounded the theme of "upward and onward."

I wanted to run away and scream. I thought at the time that we shouldn't be celebrating. At least not like this. But here, trite and superficial "worship" was the order of the day. It was God "lite." There was no mention of death, since that was definitely not victorious and happy. Music of substance in a minor key was a no-no.

A good barometer of a church is what it does with Good Friday. The average American Evangelical is taught to ignore Good Friday and to get to Sunday and the joy of the resurrection and, more important, to victory and living the Christian life. I was yearning for an honest Good Friday. My soul needed talk of sin, denial, man's hatred of God, the cross, suffering, judgment, wrath, blood, and death—all very anti-California themes. And by definition, therefore, they are also very anti-Evangelicalism themes. For all the moralism in Evangelicalism, what I yearned for was a proclamation of real Law, that I might then hear the real Gospel.

Lutheranism and the Discovery of a Christ-Centered Service

I left that "service" remembering a favorite line from the eminent death-of-God theologian Woody Allen: "God is silent. Now if we can just get man to shut up." I left looking for people who recognized their need, as it were, to "shut up" in the presence of a holy God, who saved people incapable of cooperating in the slightest degree with their own rescue.

At 7:15 that evening we loaded up the car and plodded in deathly silence toward a Lutheran church. Our expectations were not high. We just wanted Christ. We wanted content. We wanted reverence—anything but pop culture, drivel, trivia, and cute people trying to work up our emotions with cute antics.

The order of service handed to us at the door of this Lutheran church said that we were going to participate in the "ancient service of Tenebrae." The word *ancient* was one I had not heard prior to that night within the context of a Christian worship service for 20 years. Good Sign Number One.

I looked for the required high-tech light panel and sound system. It was absent. The lighting was bad. In fact, there wasn't any lighting. Just candles. Scary. But Good Sign Number Two.

I looked for the "stage" and the drum set. Absent. Good Sign Number Three.

Up front was an altar. A very big, very Roman Catholic-looking altar—one, I surmised, that might be used for those mysterious works-righteousness acts done by ministers wearing gowns. This altar had nothing on it, though, except exceedingly distressing accouterments. First, it was draped with a black piece of cloth. In fact, black was the color of choice everywhere. On the pulpit, on the lectern, and on the cross. The cross also had a crown of thorns hung on it. The architecture was definitely not conducive to being silly and frivolous. A somber, reflective mood permeated the worship space.

The pastor appeared from the back of the church dressed in a black gown. He walked slowly and in complete silence up to the altar and bowed before the cross. He did not welcome us. He did not give announcements. He did not thank us for taking time from our busy schedules to come to church. Good Signs Numbers Four, Five, and Six.

There was a medieval feel to this place. The service proceeded with a focus around the last Seven Words of Christ on the cross. After each of the seven selections were read, candles were extinguished. The pastor explained that this was being done to show the gradually increasing darkness surrounding a world that is literally killing its Redeemer.

We had confessed our sins to begin the service. That confession was as follows: "Most merciful God, we confess that we are by nature sinful and unclean. We have sinned against You in thought, word, and deed, by what we have done and by what we have left undone. We have not loved You with our whole heart; we have not loved our neighbors as ourselves. We justly deserve Your present and eternal punishment. For the sake of Your Son, Jesus Christ, have mercy on us. Forgive us, renew us, and lead us, so that we may delight in Your will and walk in Your ways to the glory of Your holy name. Amen."[1]

The confession landed a direct and staggering blow. My wife and I quickly glanced at each other in utter disbelief. This service was off to a right start. So far Lutherans were not liberal. We were acknowledging our meritlessness and our failure and rebellion and crushing the self efforts of Old Adam at achieving auto-sanctification without Christ.

The service continued until the last words of Christ were read from the Gospels. All candles were extinguished. The pastor then, in pitch darkness, startled us by dropping a very large book on the stone floor of the altar space. It resonated with the thundering crash of despondency and doom. This was to symbolize Christ being placed in the tomb and the rock rolled up against the tomb and the final cosmic despair resulting from His agonizing crucifixion. The tomb was sealed. The God-man was truly dead. We had killed Him. Not the Jews alone, but us and our sins. The sins and hatred of my family had required, and could only be atoned for by, the death of God's Son.

The pastor's voice echoed in the darkness: "Now think of how grievous your sins are that they required the death of God's highly favored and only Son. Leave in silence as you ponder the depth of your depravity." We left in holy silence. People had finally "shut up." Our efforts, our good works, our accomplishments, our skills, our kindness, our everything, had merited only the pouring out of the full wrath of God on His own Son. We left pondering the depth of our depravity. No words of brevity. No lightness. No clapping or "praising the Lord." For the first time in my memory we were being instructed to ponder our sins and their consequence.

My wife and I talked late into the night, recognizing that the service had one relentless theme—what our sins had required of the blameless Son of God. Christ as innocent Lamb had been placed in front of us in His saving office as both Priest and Sacrifice. This was a service about God's wrath and punishment poured out on a wholly innocent substitute. The spotless and holy Lamb of God slain for me. Jesus Christ had been both forsaken and punished in my place. We were overwhelmed. There was the shock of looking down into the chasm and realizing the depth of our sin. But at the same time there was the wonder of gazing up to Christ and grasping the immensity of His love and sacrifice for us.

The architectural teaching aids provided in the service were not lost on us or our children. Black altar paraments demonstrated to us the darkness of a world that mocked, spit upon, and finally crucified the Holy Savior of the world. Black indeed was our Adamic heart that by nature had willingly and gladly rebelled against God. The wooden crown of thorns reminded us of the mocking and torture that Christ had endured. But this was not the mocking of distant third-party God haters. This was *my* mocking and *my* torment of the Son of God.

The service was unapologetically disturbing and judgmental. Thus it was simultaneously anti-California and anti-Evangelical. This was the antithesis of glorifying pop culture in the church. No let up about sin and its consequences. No superficial, "happy-clappy" joy, but lots of depth. And when it was over, there were no people running up to us as visitors and extending the "right hand of fellowship" and inviting us to a potluck. No one told us of their vibrant youth group. No special music. No one in shorts and sandals. The Service of Tenebrae communicated both Law and Gospel. In the liturgy we experienced the true darkness of our sin. And in contrast we were given the complete, utter comfort of the Gospel in Christ's last words: "Father, forgive them" (Luke 23:34) and "It is finished" (John 19:30). This stood in stark contrast to Evangelicalism, where both the Law and the Gospel are watered down to a mild moralism. The Lutheran church had something else—old people. And there was somberness. There was dignity. The form of the service fit its content perfectly. No wonder it had been observed since the early Middle Ages.

The service of Tenebrae reintroduced us to a strange joy, an alien joy we had not known for years. The joy of once again hearing about biblical sin and its rightful punishment. Not the sins of others (pornographers, Democrats, Hollywood producers, abortionists, and others), but *our* sin. We tasted how deep this darkness was that had no remedy but to be met by the atoning death of the Lamb of God. This service reminded us of what we already knew we were—namely, sinners.

Not a hint of moralism came out of the pastor's mouth that night. No inane scolding about the need to be "better" or "nicer" boys and girls. This was a story about real law-breaking. Of being offensive to God. Of being given everything by a gracious Father and then despising His gifts in the most ungrateful and hostile way. This was the story of the prodigal son, only this story ended before the son had come to his senses. This was the story of the prodigal spending his inheritance on whores, grieving his father, and caring less about the consequences. Law. At last, real Law. And with it, real Gospel—the Good News of a merciful Father who indeed "justifieth the *ungodly*" (Romans 4:5 KJV, emphasis added).

To come back to that same worship space on Easter morning was to truly come back from the dead to the living. White paraments adorned the altar. Banners waved on high and proclaimed the ransom paid and sinners set free by the King of kings, who now ever lives to intercede for us. The pipe organ thundered in victory, giving evidence that it truly is the instrument of strength given as a unique gift to the church militant to fill large, enclosed spaces dedicated to the worship of the triune God. Voices were lifted in praise. The Gospel was preached. Christ's death for sin and victory over it by His resurrection for our justification was announced. Our final sanctification in Christ was secured as His merits are given to us by faith in what He accomplished on the cross. In short, we had a real Easter Sunday because for once we had first had a true Good Friday.

LUTHER'S SMALL CATECHISM AND THE RESTORATION OF A THEOLOGICALLY LITERATE LAITY

The service had evangelized us *as Christians*. From start to finish it gave us Christ. It told us of our sin and of our Savior. The service was the first completely "evangelical" service we had ever attended after becoming Christians. Christ was proclaimed as all-sufficient for the sins of Christians too.

And so we started to attend. For some time the Lutheran service remained alien to us in touch, taste, and feel. It was all very difficult to assimilate—the formal service read, chanted, and sung from a hymnal; the pipe organ with music by Bach, Mendelssohn, and Brahms in a minor key; the use of a church calendar; bowing before the cross; and confession of sin as our first words (something not at all common in California, and certainly not "seeker-friendly" as required by church-growth experts). It had a profundity and a depth that could not be immediately mastered as could the services we had been in for 20 years. It was the difference in complexity between learning a few chords on the guitar and mastering a Bach fugue on the organ. We sensed we could be moving toward a peculiar fate—becoming Roman Catholic.

What blocked that route, though, was instruction in the Scriptures. The Pastor patiently answered our questions and directed our study. He even went so far as to go through the entire Divine Service during several Sunday adult education hours and explain the biblical basis for each part of the service. Knowledge of the biblical, theological, and historical roots of the service, or liturgy,[2] led to a growing excitement and appreciation of the great gifts it so clearly and reverently proclaims, preserves, and advances within the body of Christ.[3]

We soon learned firsthand of the Lutheran church's historical commitment to serious doctrinal instruction. "Catechism Class," I had always assumed, was for Catholics and people in "dead" churches—a dead ritual for religious people and their children who were also not saved. I found out to the contrary. Luther, along with Lutheran reformers Philip Melanchthon and Johannes Bugenhagen, carefully constructed the "catechesis" or instruction of the believers at the heart of the Reformation in Wittenberg, Germany, beginning in the 1520s. The culmination of that work was Luther's Small Catechism of 1529.[4] Here the clear and systematic instruction in the essentials of Christian doctrine is set out.

We began to memorize the Ten Commandments, the Apostles' Creed, the Lord's Prayer and their evangelical meanings. We learned about distinguishing between Law and Gospel (something unknown in Evangelicalism), about the centrality of confession and forgiveness (or "absolution"), and about the sacraments of Baptism and the Lord's Supper. Every doctrine was set out with reference to biblical passages. For Lutheranism, *Non est biblicum, non est theologicum* (that which is not biblical is not theological). The Small Catechism gave us a road map to the Gospel heart of Scripture. The commandments spoke of our sin and inadequacy and pointed to the *extra nos* (outside of us; objective, alien) answer—a Christ who had perfectly fulfilled that condemning and absolute Law in thought, word, and deed. The Apostles' Creed permitted us to confess our trust in the triune God and to reflect on the threefold work of God as Creator, Redeemer, and Sanctifier. This confession leads inexorably to the life of prayer as one lives out that confession in a life of gratitude for the total rescue effected by God. Realizing that the Christian life was simply living out the doctrine of justification in a life of daily repentance and faith was as if we had rediscovered the saving Christian faith altogether.[5]

My oldest daughter began weekly instruction in Luther's Small Catechism with the pastor. This would be unheard-of in Evangelicalism where weekly meetings with a pastor are only possible if you need serious marital counseling, are generally messed up, or are under "church discipline." The classes went for two years and concluded in the ancient rite of "confirmation." Confirmation is just that—the believer publicly confesses or confirms the biblical, Christ-centered teachings he has received from the ordained minister of the Word.[6] Most Lutheran churches end the catechetical instruction with a public doctrinal examination of the students or "catechumens." Upon their biblical and evangelical confession of faith, the catechumens are "confirmed" into the full privileges and responsibilities of membership in the church militant. Most important, they are invited to partake of the Lord's Supper since they now have been instructed and publicly confess that they believe with the whole church that the Lord's true body and blood are present in, with, and under the elements of bread and wine in this sacrament (1 Corinthians 10:16–17). My daughter was welcomed into Communion at the Lord's Table to partake of His very body and blood for the forgiveness of her sins.[7]

I was struck by how profoundly pastoral Lutheran catechesis was in relation to my family. My daughter was privileged to be instructed in Christian doctrine for two hours a week for two years by a pastor who had thorough theological training. For example, Lutheran pastors are generally trained in the biblical languages of Greek and Hebrew, and many have the theological languages of Latin and German. The seminary training is rigorous— not at all like the God-called-me-out-of-being-a-general-contractor-and-now-I'm-a-pastor type of approach I had known in generic, nondenominational Evangelicalism. In many cases (such as that of our Lutheran pastor) his pre-seminary training actually began in high school with language training and was then advanced in rigorous undergraduate studies.

Strangely enough, I had had my first contact with the Small Catechism in 1982 while on staff with Campus Crusade for Christ. The book was mentioned in passing by Dr. Rosenbladt one day at the Simon Greenleaf School of Law. Later, while in Albuquerque speaking for Campus Crusade for Christ, I picked up a well-used 1943 version of the catechism. Thus, the Small Catechism began its profound effect on me 15 years before I came to Lutheranism.

First, I was struck by the clarity and conciseness of the doctrinal teaching. It majored on the majors and refused to let the student of Scripture get lost in the trees. My Evangelical background had emphasized Bible factoids (e.g., How many sons did Noah have? What were the 10 plagues called down on Pharoah? Which of David's sons committed adultery with David's concubines? How many Letters did Paul write?). The catechism went after the *sedes doctrinae* (seat of doctrine—i.e., Bible verses that establish Christian dogma).

Second, Luther's Small Catechism is the only Reformation catechism that can be prayed. It is not an exercise in the acquisition of intellectual knowledge only. It *is* clear, systematic knowledge about God. But it is more. It gives truth about ourselves and God. One profitably memorizes and speaks these biblical texts—God's Word on our lips. It is a true confession of our place before God as both sinner and saint.

Finally, the Small Catechism provided me with the clearest and most comprehensive roadmap for teaching others I had ever found. I found time-tested content and solid historical theology in the Small Catechism. Real meat. Real doctrine. My daughter's confirmation was a public examination that covered all the chief parts of the Christian faith (the Ten Commandments, the Apostles' Creed, the Lord's Prayer, the sacraments of Baptism and Holy Communion, and confession and absolution). The service was deeply moving. It was only surpassed by the service the following week when she was confirmed and received Christ's true body and blood in, with, and under the bread and wine. No such important objective forms exist in generic American Evangelicalism to mark a child's passage into adulthood within the church militant.

COMMUNIO SANCTORUM AND TEENAGERS

One daughter was just entering her teen years at this time. Mother-daughter tension was increasing in our home. I bought a male Australian shepherd dog to try and balance the atmosphere. Then we neutered him. Tension in the home was very high.

Nothing, however, helped more to remind us of our unity as Christians than receiving Christ's body and blood together in the Sacrament. There, together on our knees at the altar, we are united with the larger communion of saints—"angels and archangels and all the company of heaven" as well as all those Christians living today who confess the one true faith. We receive a Savior who ever lives to intercede for us and for our family. Our faith in Christ is increased. That is always needful, but especially so during the teen years. Communion now is the highlight of the service for all of us. This is a good and proper focus for a Christian family. When feelings about our lack of progress in the Christian life lead us to despair, we have the promise of our Lord's real presence under the bread and wine, delivering to us His salvation by His true body and blood.

We thus began our journey toward Lutheranism, first at the sorrow of Tenebrae and then the joy of Easter. We had had no experience with a church calendar, organized according to seasons and festivals, used to determine the order of service and the text for the sermon. However, we soon came to see the many benefits of following the church year. It provides a structure to assist us in hearing the whole counsel of God. The ordeal of hearing 47 straight weeks of sermons on Daniel was finally over.

But mostly we came to love the stability of a Christ-centered and thus Gospel-centered order of service. It continues to feed our hungry souls each Lord's Day with what we need, not necessarily what we want. It also provided another benefit—protection from a sermon that may not be on target every single Sunday. Regardless of how bad a sermon (or the music, or anything else) might be, one is assured that the liturgy will deliver the Word of God and Christ in His saving office. In rediscovering sin once again, we rediscovered the Gospel in all its comfort.

A Christ-centered service. Catechesis in time-tested content that centered on the essential articles of the faith. Sunday morning moved from a time of agony to a time of anticipation. At least for a season.

4

EVANGELICALISM
A MOVEMENT IN NEED
OF A CONFESSION

Lutherans are "evangelical" in the biblical sense of that word.
That is, Lutherans are formally evangelical by their doctrinal
statements, regardless of what individual Lutherans may believe.
This takes some unpacking of the words *Lutheran* and *evangelical*.

DISSECTING A LUTHERAN

Contrary to common understanding, Lutheranism is a confession and *not* a denomination. All Christians are "confessors" since
every Christian is called to point publicly to the core of his beliefs
in one way or the other.[1] It has become akin to a badge of honor
in certain megachurch Evangelical circles to have a doctrinal statement that can fit on a 3x5-inch card or, better yet, be uttered in
one sentence (e.g., "The Bible is God's Word, and Jesus died for my
sins."). Much more detail is seen as becoming overly picky about
largely irrelevant details (unless, that is, the details are about creation or the end times). *Theology* is a dirty word in Evangelicalism.
It smacks of high-brow intellectualism and a diminishing of the

life of the sanctified believer who needs only to "love the Lord."[2] Lutheranism takes an entirely different tack, which can only be understood by looking at the historical context from which the Lutheran Reformation sprang.

Though all Christians are confessors in the broad sense, Lutherans are confessional in a critical and formative sense. Luther's confrontation with Rome, commencing with the nailing of the Ninety-five Theses on the door of the Castle Church in Wittenberg in 1517, was over the center of Christian faith—how a sinner is made right with God. All other solely economic, political, or geographical interpretations of the Reformation that miss this central point simply do not understand what brought about the Reformation and what sustained it.[3] Luther and the Wittenberg reformers were required to be exceedingly clear, precise, and comprehensive in their theological position. Luther's very life depended on his position vis-à-vis official Roman doctrine. Exactly what was wrong with Rome and why it was critical. Luther was so convinced that his understanding of the Gospel and the "righteousness of God," which began to arise out of his lectures on Psalms and Romans (1513–15), was biblical that his reaction to Leo X was pure joy when Luther was informed that Leo had excommunicated him. Luther replied that the pope was not to be feared, since he would excommunicate Paul and the apostles if given the chance.[4]

Thus, out of the cauldron of persecution and excommunication, and within the context of the university, the distinctively Lutheran practice of confessing their position in writing by both affirmations and condemnations was born.[5]

Faith gives birth to confession. Trusting in our Savior displays itself in word and deed (Acts 4:20; Romans 10:9–15). Luther and the reformers became known as confessors. They were willing to put down on paper—and sign at peril of their lives—what they affirmed as biblical teaching and what they condemned as false and heretical teaching. It is thoroughly biblical to confess publicly what is true and condemn publicly what is false. The motivation for being confessional was the serious pastoral concern of Luther and the reformers that Christ's sheep learn to hear the voice of their master and also learn to discern the alluring voice of the evil one. For Luther, heaven or hell was literally at stake.

But confessions of faith divide as well as gather. They create division as well as harmony as they focus on that which must be confessed to be a Christian. As John Warwick Montgomery has often observed in his lectures, the fact that Ruth was a Moabitess is not an article of confession, not because it isn't biblical or true, but because it is not part of fundamental Christian doctrine. Because confessions seek to affirm what is true for all Christians at all times, they are "catholic" (universal). Confessions also are creedal in that they seek to be informed by what the church has always confessed publicly. That is, the historic creeds of the church are normative. They are not Scripture, but the ecumenical creeds of Christendom are to be confessed because they reflect what Scripture teaches and have the weight of 2,000 years of church history affirming that they accurately reflect Scripture. They are not true "in so far" (*quatenus*) as they reflect what Scripture says. They are true "because" (*quia*) they reflect what Scripture says.[6]

Thus the Reformation gave birth to the Lutheran church as a confessing church. The impetus for that birth was the completion by the Lutheran reformers of the Augsburg Confession of 1530. Ultimately, several more confessional statements were prepared and collected into what is known as *The Book of Concord* of 1580.[7] The title is important. The Lutheran reformers really believed they had a basis for Christian reconciliation, or "concord," as well as the refutation of heresy, in the *Book of Concord*. Since the Gospel was taught in its purity in these confessions, Christian unity—concord—was possible on the basis of the truth.

To be a confessional Lutheran is to hold to biblical doctrine as stated in the *Book of Concord*. Lutherans do not claim that the *Book of Concord* is equal to Scripture. The confessions are normed by Holy Scripture. Period. Lutherans do contend that their confessional statements correctly set forth biblical doctrine. To be ordained as a pastor in a confessional Lutheran church like the Lutheran Church—Missouri Synod, Wisconsin Evangelical Lutheran Synod, or the Evangelical Lutheran Synod, for example, one is asked publicly to profess loyalty to the Lutheran Confessions found in the *Book of Concord* as a correct and faithful exposition of the doctrine found in Scripture and to reject all the errors that they condemn.

This peculiarly Lutheran emphasis on written confessions works itself out in an exceedingly practical way, regardless of whether individual Lutherans are versed in their own confessional writings (they unfortunately often are not). The Confessions make plain what that Christian faith is that we seek to believe, teach, and defend. The basic doctrine of the Confessions becomes the possession of a Lutheran if he has been faithfully catechized or instructed by Luther's Small Catechism, since it condenses the basics of Christian doctrine into a comprehensive summary with tightly written and colorful language.

Lutherans confess because they seek to proclaim, preserve, and propagate the Word of God. By doing so, they also defend Christ's church against its enemies. Above all, Lutherans seek to confess Jesus Christ. He is head of the church. Cut off the head, and the body dies. This is why, as David Scaer says, "all theology is Christology" because all Scripture was given to point us to Christ and to salvation (John 5:39; Luke 24:44).[8] We must get the Gospel and Christ's work right and make it the center of all other doctrines. Luther makes the point bluntly: "The entire Scripture points to Christ alone."[9]

Thus the evangel, or Good News, is all about Christ's work as both priest and sacrifice. Certainly Scripture is about more. It's just that at its very core is this truth, and it must inform all theology and practice of the church. This is what a confessional Christian-

Lutheran seeks to defend, preserve, and advance. Christ's work, therefore, is the center of Lutheran theology. All doctrines flow into and out of the chief article of the church—the doctrine of justification.

The eminent historian of American Christianity, Winthrop Hudson, wrote prophetically of Lutheranism more than 30 years ago:

> The final prospect for a vigorous renewal of Protestant life and witness rests with the Lutheran Churches. . . . The Lutheran Churches are in the fortunate position of having been, in varying degrees, insulated from American life for a long period of time. As a result, they have been less subject to theological erosion, which so largely stripped other denominations of an awareness of their continuity with a historic Christian tradition. Thus the resources of the Christian past have been more readily available to them, and this fact suggests that they may have an increasingly important role to play in a Protestant recovery. Among the assets immediately at hand among the Lutherans are a confessional tradition, a surviving liturgical structure, and a sense of community which, however much it may be of cultural factors, may make it easier for them than most Protestant denominations to recover the integrity of church membership without which Protestants are ill-equipped to participate effectively in the dialogue of a pluralistic society.[10]

Evangelicalism is a movement in need of a confession that puts that evangel once again at the center of its doctrine and practice. It needs to learn from Lutheranism. Lutheranism needs to become the teacher of Evangelicalism, and not the pupil. Perhaps then Lutheranism will assist in the rescue of the evangel from a deteriorating Evangelicalism.

> Before turning to a consideration of apologetics, we must note at the outset that the enterprise of defending the faith has its limits—as do all human attempts to evangelize. Apologetics endeavors to remove intellectual obstacles from the mind of

the skeptic, thus preparing the way for the evangelistic proclamation of a gracious God in Christ who forgives sin to those
who repent. But neither the apologist nor the evangelist "converts"—only the Holy Spirit can do that. Apologetics can convince in the realm of reason, historicity, and verifiable facts, but
"faith comes from hearing, and hearing through the word of
Christ" (Romans 10:17, ESV).

In an age such as ours, where the Christian faith is everywhere
opposed by secular and religious philosophies, it is important
for us to engage the skeptics in the marketplace of ideas. The
apologist shows the doubter that the Christian faith rests on a
solid basis of evidence—its convincing force is as we say in
trial law, "beyond a reasonable doubt." Indeed, the average
believer today will frequently encounter in the workplace or
at college or over the backyard fence a mind that just assumes
that the Bible is full of errors and contradictions or that the
resurrection of Jesus was made up by the gullible and biased
members of the early church. It's in the cultural atmosphere.
To the open inquirer the apologist can set forth reasonable and
convincing evidence for the truth claims of the Christian
faith, as well as point him to the artistic, literary, and musical
treasures of the one, holy, catholic, and apostolic church. To be
sure, once convinced, the former doubter is not yet saved.
Now Law and Gospel must be proclaimed. But in today's cultural climate, the apologist is needed more than ever. Readers
of this book will perhaps be surprised to find that Lutheran
theology and practice provide not only that clear proclamation
of the Gospel but also the best basis for a recovery of a Christocentric apologetic.[11]

5

A LUTHERAN DEFENSE OF THE BIBLICAL GOSPEL

The unique contribution of Lutheranism is in going to the heart of Scripture, that is, to Christ, and in having both its doctrine and its worship center on Christ. This in turn has profound application to apologetics, the defense of the Christian faith. A Lutheran apologetic will therefore defend that which is central to the faith—Christ crucified for sinners and resurrected from the dead for their justification. All biblical apologetics will ultimately be Christocentric.

Compare this to other approaches that see justification just as one among many Christian doctrines. It is not surprising that both Roman Catholic Thomism and Calvinist orthodoxy, both beginning with God in eternity, have generated a long tradition of philosophical defenses of the faith centering on evidences for the existence of God.[1] Such efforts have much value, and any serious apologist will certainly be acquainted with these arguments and their advantages. But a Lutheran defense of the faith will have a riveted and unflinching focus on the cross. Before we look at that apologetic, we first want to answer objections raised by Lutherans themselves and others to the apologetical task.

DEFENDING THE DEFENSE
OF THE FAITH AMONG LUTHERANS

Some orthodox Lutherans have decried any effort at developing an apologetic that advocates reasoning with the unbeliever who is dead in sin. It is argued that evidential apologetics just feeds the pride of the Old Adam in making him think that he can, on his own, believe the evidences for Christian faith. In addition, didn't Luther call reason the "devil's whore," thus renouncing all efforts to give the unbeliever the idea that he cooperated with God in salvation? Luther's Small Catechism clearly says that "I cannot by my own reason or strength believe in Jesus Christ, my Lord, or come to Him."[2]

We are by no means suggesting that man, without the work of the Holy Spirit through the preached Gospel, can cooperate with God and achieve a self-generated salvation as the heretic Pelagius taught. Indeed, man was corrupted by the fall (will, emotions, and intellect) and is "totally depraved." But man did not lose his inferential faculties at the fall. Man did not become non-man. Thus man can still understand facts and can still interpret those facts correctly.[3] While there is a tendency to minimize reason in some Lutheran circles, the evidence shows that Luther himself appreciated the use of reason within its proper sphere.[4]

Moreover, the apostolic preaching of Paul does not take such a jaundiced view of fallen man's ability to understand the biblical data concerning Christ. Because Paul preached those facts as real facts in history that could be checked out by the unbeliever does not mean he denied that salvation is *sola gratia* and *sola fide*.

As for Luther, he certainly railed against reason as the devil's whore. But what "reason" was Luther referencing? Surely not man's inferential capacities, for Luther clearly understood that the fall had not obliterated man's ability to discover truth in all fields of learning. No, what Luther railed against was any use of reason to achieve salvation or to allow the unbeliever, by his own striving, to climb up to heaven.[5] Some may counter that the unbeliever can discover "secular" facts and interpret them correctly (after all, even a pagan medical doctor can correctly diagnose cancer), but he certainly cannot discover or correctly interpret any fact that has anything to do with the Gospel of Jesus Christ.

This argument is ultimately refuted in the doctrine of the incarnation, however, which is at the center of Lutheran teaching. If Lutheranism is anything, it is incarnational—fleshly and sacramental. God became man. Mary gave birth to Him who made her. There are no "spiritual" facts in the Bible. There are just facts. But it is also true that human reason can never generate personal trust in the facts that lie at the heart of the Gospel (i.e., that the death of Jesus Christ was for the sins of the world, and His resurrection for its justification). We can prove factually that Jesus died on a cross. But that does not mean that the skeptic will believe and be saved.[6] The Apostles' Creed knows of no such division or separation of facts into historical and spiritual realms, mentioning the secular official Pontius Pilate right alongside central facts such as the resurrection and the virgin birth.[7] The evangelist Luke announces the virgin birth as occurring "while Quirinius was governor of Syria" (Luke 2:2).

We have looked at the structure of Lutheranism and found that it is confessional and Christocentric. Now we want to see what a Lutheran defense of the biblical Gospel will look like. We also want to bring an additional perspective to bear on the defense of the Gospel. We want to find out how the legal profession can assist in the defense of the faith and why the objective and evidential perspective of legal reasoning is perfectly suited to complement a Lutheran defense of the objective biblical Gospel in a relativistic, postmodern age.

WHY APOLOGETICS HAS BECOME AN ENDANGERED SPECIES IN THE CHURCH

After a series of lectures I recently delivered on law, lawyers, and the legal defense of the biblical Gospel at an Evangelical college, a student raised an issue that was troubling her: "Though I don't doubt these evidences, they seem to take away the need for faith. Faith doesn't need evidence. Isn't faith believing in spite of the evidence?" This student verbalized a standard argument against the apologetical task and a tension sensed by Christians in every age: that between faith and reason, between knowing and believing, between head knowledge and heart commitment. Though we have briefly touched upon certain Lutheran objections to apologetics, we now examine important criticisms, then look at the biblical basis for the apologetical task.

Apologetics, a branch of theology interested in the defense of Christian truth claims, is an unwanted guest in many Christian churches. It is often ignored, despised, or totally unknown. Traditionally, apologetics was one of the three main branches of systematic theology and a standard course in seminary training. Today apologetics is rarely even offered in standard seminary curricula. This is particularly disturbing in light of the conflicts within Christendom (in the widest sense)—between orthodox theologians on the one hand and the advocates of liberalism and neo-orthodoxy on the other. When the attacks of rank unbelief upon Christianity are added to the mix (cults, non-Christian religions, New Age movements, humanistic philosophical systems, etc.), it is staggering that so few theologians show any serious competency in the area.

To the contrary, apologists are often viewed as unspiritual "intellectual types" who sacrifice a heart relationship with the Lord for the academic pursuit of knowledge. It is often perceived that the apologist is either answering questions no one is asking or is attempting to "prove" that which must be accepted by faith. Most interestingly, almost none of the most effective apologists in the twentieth century have had professional training in formal theology. One thinks immediately of C. S. Lewis, J. R. R. Tolkien, G. K. Chesterton, Dorothy Sayers, Charles Williams, and T. S. Eliot. Perhaps training in other disciplines outside theology, where rigorous external proofs and reasoning are required, is the best preparation for speaking to unbelievers. How many unbelievers actually read works by systematic theologians or dogmaticians? Precious few, if any. But the unbeliever does read Lewis, Tolkien, and Sayers when they write on the defense of the Christian faith because they made their mark first in areas of study outside theology (in the case of these three, English literature).

First, let's examine the common theological positions (Protestant liberalism, neo-orthodoxy of Karl Barth and de-mythologizing of Rudolf Bultmann, and misguided orthodoxy) that object to apologetics in our effort to discover why so few are concerned with the biblical command to "contend for the faith" (Jude 3).

PROTESTANT LIBERALISM:
A CHRISTIANITY WITHOUT A CROSS

The modern-day liberal Christian is classically portrayed in John Updike's novel *Rabbit Run* or as the minister in the film *Simon Birch*. Willard L. Sperry's book *Yes, But—: The Bankruptcy of Apologetics*[8] made explicit liberalism's annoyance with apologetics. Sperry chided all attempts to argue for biblical truth over and against the proven axioms of science. If science spoke on a topic covered by the Bible and by theology, then Scripture was to listen. If science contradicted Scripture, too bad for Scripture. The only sane response of Christians, said the liberals, was to agree with the findings of science and to either reject the teaching of the Scripture or attempt to accommodate the biblical material to scientific findings.

Underlying Protestant liberalism are two basic assumptions: First, Christianity is not about objective, propositional statements of truth but is a call to a new life and to social action (the "Social Gospel"). Second, liberals like Sperry believed that Christianity was really not qualitatively different from other religions. Since all religions are headed up the same mountain, efforts at convincing others of the errors of their ways is wholly misguided.

Liberalism, as is now generally recognized in credible scholarly and theological circles, has a thoroughly discredited view of Christian truth claims. It simply cannot maintain its position in light of the actual New Testament historical record. Those records present the Christian faith as a matter of concrete, propositional truth claims. Christ Himself makes this clear ("Believe Me when I say that I am in the Father and the Father is in Me"—John 14:11), as do the creedal affirmations of the apostles in the New Testament ("For what I received I passed on to you as of first importance: that Christ died for our sins according to the Scriptures . . . that He was raised on the third day according to the Scriptures"—1 Corinthians 15:3–4). Christianity is not, ultimately, a matter of feeling or emotion or social action. Christianity yields feelings and emotion and social action only because it is a faith founded on fact. The objective, factual truth claims of Christianity are the only basis for the subjective experience and social action that result from its truth. As for the argument that all paths lead up the same mountain, the Jesus of the primary source documents will simply have none of it ("I am the way and the truth and the life. No one comes to the Father except through Me"—John 14:6) and the apostles decimate the view ("There is no other name under heaven given to men by which we must be saved"—Acts 4:12).

Liberalism's despising of apologetics is thus seen for what it is— the rejection of the Christian faith. The religious liberal is left with a subjective religious feeling that is created in his own vain image and is utterly divorced from the New Testament record. Christianity needs no defense in liberalism because liberal Christianity is a nonfactual "faith" position based solely on the "teachings of love" given by Christ. They want a Christ who did not "suffer under Pontius Pilate." This denial however, as the lay Roman Catholic theologian and member of the French Academy Jean Guitton points out, is the most basic heresy of all.[9]

BARTH AND BULTMANN: "FIXING" AN ORTHODOXY THAT WAS NEVER BROKEN

The Swiss theologian Karl Barth is justly praised for bringing down Protestant modernism. Barth, however, disliked apologetics as much as the modernists. While he defended the basic Christian verities as objectively true, he sealed these events off in a special realm of history not testable for the seeking unbeliever.

It has been noted that early in his career Barth asserted that the miraculous events of the Gospel (like the virgin birth, the resurrection, etc.) took place in *Geschichte,* or "meta" history—a realm not subject to the ordinary canons of historical inquiry. In later writings Barth preferred not to make this distinction but still took the position that the miraculous events in Scripture cannot be verified absent a prior belief in those events.[10] Thus for Barth neither Scripture nor the saving events contained therein can be "proven" to the unbeliever. Only by the individual's faith can the Bible take its place as (i.e., become for me) the verifiable Word of God. This leaves the "biblical witness" of the saving events altogether out of the conversation with an unbeliever.

Rudolph Bultmann and his disciples took the train of thought started by Barth and drove it to its logical culmination. For Bultmann, the objective events in Scripture are not the essence of the Christian message. No, the biblical miracles are not only secondary, they are irrelevant when compared to the existential encounter with the Christ they proclaim. The New Testament, in fact, must be "demythologized" so as to get at its core message of the subjective, existential experience of salvation. Rather than the proclamation of what has objectively happened in the past at Calvary, Christianity for Bultmann is the experience of Christ in the present possible through "personal encounter."[11]

Barth and Bultmann both distrusted apologetics but for different reasons. For Barth, the objective facts of biblical history could not be subject to verification since that could lead to doubt as to their veracity. Barth accepted the underpinnings and basic validity of the higher critical school of biblical analysis. If scholars of literature and history were allowed to attack the saving events of Scripture, the result would be the loss of faith. Thus those saving events were walled off in a special realm of history where objective historical investigation might not intrude. For Bultmann, the distrust of the reliability of the Scripture as historically verifiable fact resulted in losing those events as significant in any sense. All that was left was an existential, subjective encounter with Christ. But without any objective historical referent, how does one know that one is encountering Christ and not indigestion? More important, Scripture itself proclaims that the "Word became flesh" (John 1:14) and that the factual nature of the resurrection could convince even the faithless (John 20:24–29) and that "none of this" (i.e., the life, death, and resurrection of Christ) was done in a hermetically sealed corner of history (Acts 26:26).

Contrary to Barth and Bultmann, it is not the defense of the faith that makes it irrelevant to the unbeliever, but the *failure* to defend the faith. Barth offered a Christ in a history not capable of verification, while Bultmann called pagans to encounter a Christ of his own subjective creation utterly divorced from the objective Word. The incarnation refutes Barth (Christ was born "while Quirinius was governor of Syria"—Luke 2:2). As for Bultmann, Festus tried out some Bultmannian theology on the apostle Paul in an effort to discount the resurrection, arguing that Paul's interior life (Paul's "great learning"—Acts 26:24) explained the whole resurrection story as the subjective meanderings of a madman. The apostle would have none of it and refused to let the whole argument degenerate to a subjective "life story."[12]

Orthodox Objections to Apologetics: With Friends Like This, Who Needs Enemies?

Two other camps of Christian believers also oppose apologetics, though for different reasons. These orthodox objections to apologetics are the presuppositionalists and the fideists. Both hold to the authority of Scripture and the total historicity of the saving events of Scripture. Thus they condemn both Barth and Bultmann categorically.

The presuppositionalist argues that because of the fall, a radical cleavage exists between the world of the believer and that of the unbeliever. This cleavage is so distinct and enormous that the Christian cannot convince the unbeliever of the truth of Christianity. Some presuppositionalists go so far as to say that the unbeliever cannot even discover secular facts, others say that he can discover secular facts but cannot interpret those facts correctly, and still others say that he cannot discover revelational facts nor interpret them correctly. Whatever the variety, presuppositionalists agree that the unbeliever cannot interpret the saving truths of Scripture correctly and thus the apologetical task is futile. It is worthless to try to persuade the unbeliever since he will inevitably twist the facts to fit his own Adamic presuppositions. A wall exists between the believer and the unbeliever, and no amount of rational argument can even begin to address the unbelief or the reasons for it in order to break it down.

The other "orthodox" objection to apologetics comes from the fideist who argues that it is unspiritual to even attempt to reason with the unbeliever and to show him the truth of the Christian faith. Only the preaching of the Gospel should be engaged in, and any attempt to argue with the pagan is to substitute human reason for the work of the Holy Spirit. As previously noted, some Lutherans misread Luther on this point.

Note immediately that the objections of the orthodox strike much deeper than those of the modernist or neo-orthodox. First of all, the orthodox take Scripture seriously and place confidence in the saving power of the Gospel. But note: both orthodox objections reflect a faulty view of the fall and the result of man's rebellion against God. Man did not lose his inferential capacities at the fall, though they were thoroughly tainted by sin. He did lose any ability to reason himself into heaven or to merit God's favor by his use of that reason. The university is predicated on the assumption that human knowledge advances through the discovery of truth and that human reason can discover truth. Pagans can write scholarly historical accounts, can discover cures for diseases, and can paint or compose great works of beauty and majesty. Academia is built on the idea that people can learn truth and that minds are changed when truth is encountered. A sign of maturity is to change one's beliefs when truth is encountered.

The moment the Christian sequesters the life, death, and resurrection of Christ into a hermetically sealed world that the unbeliever may not enter, he divorces Christianity from its incarnational moorings. Whatever else such a Christian may be defending, it is *not* biblical Christianity. If the unbeliever can be helped to see that Christ rose again in the same history where Napoléon met his Waterloo, then he can also be assisted to see that alternate "interpretations" of the resurrection are not all equally valid. Facts determine interpretations, and the best interpretation of an event is the one that has the most comprehensive view of the facts.[13] When the unbeliever tries to distort those facts, refuses to face those facts, or imposes gratuitous interpretations unsupported by those facts, the Christian apologist can guide the discussion back to the historical record. Not all interpretations are equal, and we hardly abrogate the work of the Holy Spirit when we point this out to the unbeliever.

THE APOSTLES AND APOLOGETICS: THE WORK OF BIBLICAL MISSIONS

Any effective missionary is a good apologist. Why? Because missionaries seek to preach Christ crucified to the culture they are operating in at the time. That culture will present unique obstacles to the Gospel—obstacles that must be destroyed by effective apologetical work so that the unbeliever in that culture is faced with the only true offense: the offense of the cross. Effective apologetics means that all pseudo-obstacles to the cross are laid waste so that the unbeliever sees the options starkly and either attempts to save himself (through merit, mysticism, or rationalism[14]) or cries out to the Lord Jesus Christ: "Lord, have mercy on me, for I am a sinner." Apologetics seeks to remove intellectual obstacles so that an unbeliever can be confronted with the real obstacle: Jesus Christ, the only legitimate "stumbling block" (1 Corinthians 1:23). Once objections are dealt with, we proclaim the Law that convicts of sin and the Gospel that forgives sin.

But does the New Testament itself support such an approach to preaching Christ? Didn't the apostles simply preach and not try to reason or do apologetics? We need go no further than Doubting (actually *unbelieving* in the Greek) Thomas to see how our Lord deals with the need for empirical verification. While others relied on the testimony of eyewitnesses (and Thomas was properly chastised by the Lord for not believing that reliable eyewitness testimony—see John 20:24–29), the Lord granted Thomas's request for tactile proof of His resurrection. Thomas's response was swift: "My Lord and my God."

Acts 17 provides the classic confrontation between Paul and the Stoic and Epicurean philosophers of Athens. The Epicureans were both self-indulgent and cynical—the Sadducees of the Greeks, says R. C. H. Lenski.[15] Paul, therefore, aimed his apologetical efforts at the Stoics, showing more than average facility with classical Stoic poets as he quotes Cleanthes, Aratus, and Epimenides. Though these poets reflected a longing for God expressed culturally by the Athenians in their statue to "an unknown God," Paul moves from where they are to where they must go—namely, the resurrection of Christ (Acts 17:31). In the end, Paul proclaimed the Christ he knew some would scoff at. Richard Longenecker points out that Paul's desire to "be all things to all men that by all means some might be saved" (1 Corinthians 9:22) is the key to his entire ministry.[16] Like his Lord, Paul sought out unbelievers in order to warn them of the peril to come. Christ Himself was known as a "friend of . . . 'sinners'" (Matthew 11:19; Luke 7:34) and had the harshest words for religious people who considered themselves in no need of a spiritual physician.

Unlike the liberal Christian, neo-orthodox Christian, and misguided orthodox Christian, Paul and our Lord placed the fact of the incarnation in front of their pagan hearers.[17] Paul challenged Festus to examine the objective evidence of the resurrection ("it was not done in a corner"—Acts 26:26), Luke argued on the basis of "many convincing proofs" (Acts 1:3), and Peter challenges us by the Holy Spirit to "always be prepared to give an answer [Greek, *apologia*] to everyone who asks you to give the reason for the hope that you have" (1 Peter 3:15). John Warwick Montgomery sums it up well: "The church of the New Testament is not an esoteric, occult, gnostic sect whose teachings are demonstrable only to initiates; it is the religion of the incarnate God, at whose death the veil of the temple was rent from top to bottom, opening holy truth to all who would seek it."[18]

APOLOGETICS IN A DOT-COM WORLD

The age of unbelief we live in is strikingly similar to that which confronted the first disciples. We are now into a third century of secularism, and it is not uncommon to find people utterly ignorant of even basic Bible knowledge. Raw paganism is often the order of the day, with violence, hedonism, and athletic prowess the objects of the new idolatry. Pluralism flourishes, and Christianity is forced to compete in the world of ideas with utterly no institutional advantages such as it had under the Holy Roman Empire (or has today under governments such as England that at least in principle are Christian in nature and do not observe a separation of church and state).

In such a pluralistic situation how exactly is the unbeliever to arbitrate between competing claims to truth? Is he to line up all the non-Christian philosophies in alphabetical order, try them one by one until they fail, and then finally ultimately stumble onto Christianity? The unbeliever must, under such an approach, first try agnosticism, atheism, Baha'i and Buddhism (both Mahayana and Hinayana varietals) before coming to Christianity. Well-known writer Arthur Koestler is a particularly poignant example of what happens to the human psyche under such an approach. Koestler tried Communism as well as Eastern mysticism. It took Koestler almost 10 years to extricate himself from Communism[19] and another long stint before the utter selfishness and paganism of Eastern mysticism became clear.[20]

Christians do the Gospel no favors by proclaiming a try-it-you'll-like-it approach. Yet this is precisely what much of moralistic Evangelicalism is about: Jesus gives happier homes, helps you lose weight, and gives you the power to smile when you learn that your family has just been burned up in a plane accident. To add to the misery, those Christians inclined to appreciate the apologetical task are given supposed theological reasons *not* to defend the faith with evidence to the unbeliever. Calvinist presuppositionalists (which, sadly enough, also influence some Lutherans) have emasculated serious apologetical activity among pagans. By arguing that their system is more "self-consistent" than that of the pagan, and by spending their apologetical time refuting non-Christian belief systems, the presuppositionalists forget two critical points: First, consistency does not mean that you have divine revelation. Euclid produced a perfectly consistent system of geometry and Marx arguably developed an internally consistent theory of history based on a materialistic metaphysic (i.e., one based on economic factors alone), but one would hardly claim that either rises to the level of divine revelation. Second, the refutation of non-Christian belief systems, while necessary, does not *ipso facto* establish the truth of Christianity. In addition, the refutation of every non-Christian alternative would consume a lifetime.

Anthony Flew, the analytical philosopher, has developed a parable that illustrates the utter meaninglessness of religious philosophies that refuse to submit to evidential scrutiny:

> Once upon a time two explorers came upon a clearing in the jungle. In the clearing were growing many flowers and many weeds. One explorer says, "Some gardener must tend this plot." The other disagrees, "There is no gardener." So they pitch their tents and set a watch. No gardener is ever seen. "But perhaps he is an invisible gardener." So they set up a barbed-wire fence. They electrify it. They patrol with bloodhounds. (For they remember how H. G. Wells' *The Invisible Man* could be both smelt and touched though he could not be seen.) But no shrieks ever suggest that some intruder has received a shock. No movements of the wire ever betray an invisible climber. The bloodhounds never give cry. Yet still the Believer is not convinced. "But there is a gardener, invisible, insensible to electric shocks, a gardener who has no scent and makes no sound, a gardener who comes secretly to look after the garden which he loves." At last the Sceptic despairs, "But what remains of your original assertion? Just how does what you call an invisible, intangible, eternally elusive gardener differ from an imaginary gardener or even no gardener at all?"[21]

This parable might seem to render devastating judgment on all attempts to present religious or ultimate claims that cannot in principle be verified by objective referents. After all, no facts in principle could refute the Believer in the Flew parable. To be sure, this is a damning judgment on all non-Christian positions. But what of the Christian position? Christianity stands unique in that it rises and falls on the facticity of one event. It shows us One who was mistaken for a gardener, but who was in fact the risen Christ. Refute this event factually (or by producing the corpse) and it utterly falls. The apostle Paul himself warns that Christianity is utterly pernicious if Christ has not indeed risen from the dead (1 Corinthians 15:12–19). If Christ be not raised, says Paul, we have been found to be liars about this life and the next. Even darker, we are still in our sins. Paul's entire apologetic is built on the facticity and objectivity of the resurrection—an event that can be verified by all serious seekers of the truth. Once this is established, then it is time to preach this risen Christ, who gladly went the way of death for sinners.

WHY DISTRUST OF EVIDENTIAL APOLOGETICS IS NOT LUTHERAN

But is orthodoxy really hostile to the evidential apologetical approach? In particular we must ask: Is orthodox Lutheranism antithetical to apologetics? If Luther's view of reason as the devil's whore is really the whole picture, isn't this a damning judgment on all efforts at persuasion based on revelational facts?

Luther was not against apologetics. He was, however, exceedingly careful about his starting point in the apologetical task. While he assumes the existence of God—which even today many non-Christian seekers will also grant—Luther insists on moving to the connecting link between earth and heaven, namely, at the point of the incarnation:

> If you begin your study of God by trying to determine how He rules the world, how He burned Sodom and Gomorrah with infernal fire, whether He has elected this person or that, and thus begin with the works of the High Majesty, then you will presently break your neck and be hurled from heaven, suffering a fall like Lucifer's. For such procedure amounts to beginning on top and building the roof before you have laid the foundation. Therefore, letting God do whatever He is doing, you must begin at the bottom and say: I do not want to know God until I have first known this Man; for so read the passages of Scripture: "I am the Way, the Truth, and the Life"; again: "No man cometh unto the Father but by Me" (John 14:6). And there are more passages to the same effect.[22]

It is true that Luther never built a formal apologetical approach from an incarnational starting point. The reason is obvious: none of

Luther's opponents contested the incarnation or the fact of the resurrection. Some of the most important of Luther's interpreters, however, give the impression that the reformer's stress on the two kingdoms meant that reason and proof only operate in the secular realm of this world but are of no heavenly value.[23] In point of fact, Luther's position is that reason operates in both kingdoms, but in the church reason is to be subservient to the Word of God. In the Christian faith, reason must operate ministerially, not magisterially.

It is accurate to say that Luther considered the distinction between the two kingdoms of utmost value and importance to his entire theology. But a deeper analysis shows that Luther places the critical point of contact at two places: First, in the incarnation of Christ in real history and, second, in the life of the individual Christian.[24] He grounds his entire comfort in the fact that the Gospel was objectively true and entirely *extra nos*. Luther's proclamation of the Gospel was based on the revealed facts. This supports an approach to apologetics that is evidential and fact-driven. One must always go from the outward to the inward in the Christian life, never allowing subjective experience to consume the presentation of the objective Gospel to the unbeliever. This approach would provide the basis for later Lutheran dogmaticians to emphasize that *notitia* (knowledge based on objective fact) must always ground *fiducia* (faith, or personal trust). That heartfelt commitment always and only flows out of the Gospel that is objectively true.

Thus we see that at its center Luther's theology is cross-centered, objective, and verifiable in the most critical sense of the word. Indeed, in his historic confrontation at the Diet of Worms Luther staked his very life on the objectivity of the Word of God and its objective sense. Luther was not against apologetics—he was, though, a student of Holy Writ who worked with the Scriptures inductively, refusing to impose from the top down interpretations that appeared logical and consistent. This was particularly evident at the Marburg Colloquy in Luther's arguments with Zwingli over the nature of the sacraments. Zwingli (and later the Calvinists), beginning with the philosophical principle *finitum non capax infiniti* (the finite is not capable of the infinite), insisted that the real presence of Christ in the sacrament of Holy Communion was a logical impossibility. That is, a finite element such as bread could not contain God. Luther, who had already stated at the Diet of Worms that his conscience was captive to the Word of God, insisted on the plain, literal sense of the text where Jesus says, "This is My body," even though in so doing Scripture presents a logical dilemma: *finitum est capax infiniti* (the finite is capable of the infinite). Luther's sacramental theology was built from the bottom up. It is a biblical theology based on an inductive methodology that, as John Warwick Montgomery has plainly shown, planted the seed for the blossoming of scientific inquiry during the Reformation and thereafter.[25]

Rather than setting a foundation for the destruction of apologetics, Luther instead provides the most solid epistemological basis for the task in being objective and inductive. If any further proof of this is required, one only need look at the apologetical work of the seventeenth-century Lutheran dogmaticians. Even Christian existentialists like Jaroslav Pelikan have to admit that essentially every name in Lutheran dogmatics from Luther to the eighteenth-century present in their *Loci Theologici* an objective apologetic, a defense of the faith, and an appeal to so-called "natural theology."[26]

Thus at the end of the day we can say that Luther, rather than casting doubt on the apologetical task, provides us with the surest foundation for making that effort Christocentric, cross-driven, and objectively centered. Luther would not let human reason think it could save itself by speculations or by rational deductions or philosophizing. But God gave us a reason that remains capable of determining if events in history really occurred. Believer and unbeliever can determine facts. Of course this is not yet saving faith. Those same facts carry with them the proper interpretation. Data always precede interpretations. The best interpretations are those that bubble up from the text (or event) itself that is being investigated. Thus the Christian may lead the mind of the seeker to the conclusion that the witness of Scripture is reliable, in preparation for leading him or her to Christ. The biblical Gospel presents facts that can be investigated and found to be true by use of the same historical inquiry used to determine if Charlemagne was crowned Holy Roman Emperor at Aachen in A.D. 800. As we shall see, the consequence of the facts of the biblical Gospel being true are enormously more significant than the consequences flowing from Charlemagne being found to actually have been crowned Holy Roman Emperor at that time. My eternal destiny does not depend on where I stand on Charlemagne. The point, however, is that the same historical inquiry is conducted as to Charlemagne as it is with the death and resurrection of Jesus Christ. The consequences of those facts being true and verifiable are obviously radically different depending on the claims verified during the historical investigation.

6

LAW, LAWYERS, LUTHERANISM, AND THE LEGAL DEFENSE OF THE BIBLICAL GOSPEL

We have seen how Christianity is qualitatively different from all other claims to religious truth. For example, Eastern religions ask the inquirer to enter into the experience of the religion, for by doing so, they say, one will find the position to be self-validating. Islam does the same. In other words, if you just submit to Allah and become a Muslim, the religion will all make sense to you. But as analytical philosopher Kai Nielson and others have shown, such subjective experientialism is utterly, and logically, incapable of validating any resulting "God-talk."[1]

Thus all non-Christian religious positions suffer from the same flaw: untestability. But as the analytical philosophers have taken pains to show, any claim that is not at least in principle subject to falsification is technically meaningless. Christianity, however, stands in stark contrast to such meaningless assertions for as the apostle Paul states, "if Christ has not been raised," we have been found to be liars about the nature of God and the Christian faith is worthless and dangerous because it operates as a deception (1 Corinthians 15:12–19). Christianity *is* falsifiable in principle, for if the body of Christ was discovered and it could be verified to be that body, the Christian position totally collapses under the weight of its own admission.

Ogden Nash's marvelous poem "The Seven Spiritual Ages of Mrs. Marmeduke Moore" points out what happens when modern seekers attempt to experience religious truth before checking out the evidence for the position. Mrs. Marmeduke Moore goes from one ultimate and riveting religious experience to another—from high Anglicanism to feminism to Eastern mysticism. Like Arthur Koestler, the fictional Mrs. Marmeduke Moore is quintessentially modern—for her, truth questions are secondary to issues of experience. What Nash makes clear is that Mrs. Marmeduke Moore wouldn't know truth if it hit her on the head. She ends up so jaded by her experiences that she is essentially incapacitated from discovering truth. All religious truth claims must be investigated and verified or falsified. Lawyers can help in this critical task.

PRIESTS IN NEED OF LAWYERS: WHAT THEOLOGY CAN LEARN FROM THE LAW

Lawyers aren't known for letting their emotions run away with them. Yet lawyers have been some of the ablest advocates of Christian truth claims and have produced some of the most substantial works in defense of the faith—works that have received a much wider reading than the voluminous works of systematic theology. It is useful to ask why we may look at the law (as opposed to dentistry, for example) as a profession from which the apologetical task has much to learn.

First, lawyers are about the last group in society that can be said to have a bias in favor of religion. Today's current view of lawyers ranks them somewhere below politicians and slightly above used-car salesmen in terms of moral or religious sensibilities. So if we study how lawyers have investigated and become convinced of

Christian truth claims, we will not likely assume or conclude that lawyers are naturally religious and more sensitive to spiritual things. If there is one group whom you would guess would *not* want the concept of a last judgment to be true, it would be lawyers. And second, the legal profession has spent considerable time developing and sharpening the mechanisms by which factual issues are unbiasedly investigated and resolved without the use of force. Any lawyer who has taken the California Bar Exam, for example, can attest to the layers of complexity built into the hearsay evidence rule in that state. Lawyers are necessarily involved in the resolution of factual disputes since factual issues always underlie legal issues. It is the application of the sophisticated evidential machinery assembled by the law to which we will now turn our attention.

LAWYERS IN DEFENSE OF THE BIBLICAL GOSPEL

Contrary to what one might believe is the case, lawyers have been some of the strongest advocates of Christian truth claims. For example, the "Father of International Law" is Hugo Grotius. Grotius was a seventeenth-century Dutchman who wrote the great work on international law entitled *De Jure Bellum Pacis*—On the Law of War and Peace. It is less well known, however, that Grotius wrote the first modern textbook on Christian apologetics *(De Veritate Religiones Christianae[2]),* published in 1623. In that work Grotius marshals the evidence for the resurrection and subjects the claims of the eyewitnesses to the resurrection to cross-examination. Similarly, Sir Matthew Hale, Lord High Chancellor under Charles V, wrote in defense of the Christian faith.

In the nineteenth century Simon Greenleaf, professor of evidence at Harvard and the greatest living scholar on evidence at the time, turned his professional skills toward an investigation of the veracity of the Gospel writers. Greenleaf's work, *The Testimony of the Evangelists,*[3] remains a classic in the field of apologetics. Greenleaf concludes by finding that the Gospel writers withstand the most rigorous scrutiny and that their eyewitness testimony would be admissible in any court of law in the country. Along with being president of the Massachusetts Bible Society, Greenleaf was able to advance his interest in world missions by helping to draft the original constitution for the new nation of Liberia.

In our own time, Lord Hailsham, former high chancellor of England, moved from unbelief (though baptized an Anglican) to Christianity on the basis of his investigation of the evidence for Christian faith. Hailsham has done significant work on pagan sources for the life of Christ.[4] Similarly, Sir Norman Anderson is widely recognized as the greatest authority on Islamic law outside the Muslim world. For many years he was professor of oriental law and director of the Institute of Advanced Legal Studies at the University of London. Professor Anderson has written on the importance of legal analysis and factual inquiry when dealing with religious claims and has brought his considerable skill in legal evidences to the case for the resurrection of Christ.[5] On the continent, Jacques Ellul, professor of law at the University of Bordeaux, has analyzed the sociology of religious experience and argued powerfully for restoration of biblically grounded absolutes within the public square.[6]

Finally, Dr. John Warwick Montgomery is the foremost living advocate of evidential and legal apologetics. Former professor of law and humanities at the University of Luton in England, Montgomery holds 10 earned degrees and is an American attorney and an English barrister (Middle Temple, Lincoln's Inn). Author of more than 50 books on law, apologetics, theology, philosophy, history, and the occult, Montgomery is ordained in the Lutheran Church—Missouri Synod. His debates with the likes of situation ethicist Joseph Fletcher, death-of-God advocate Thomas J. J. Altizer, infamous atheist Madeline Murray O'Hare, and heretic Bishop James Pike are historic.[7] Montgomery's colorful personality (he is a member of the prestigious *Academie des Gourmetts et des Tra-*

ditions Gastronomiques de Paris [almost unheard-of for Americans] as well as a member of the Sherlock Holmes Society of London) and his commitment to bringing the transcendental perspective of the inerrant Word of God found only in the Holy Scriptures to the major human rights issues of our day make him unique among Christian apologists.

What is it about Christian truth that has attracted such a diverse group of legally trained professionals? The answer by now should be plain: nothing short of the sheer objectivity of Christian truth claims and the factual character of those claims makes Christian faith so appealing to the legally trained advocate. Lawyers are necessarily concerned with facts and the reliability of evidence. Lawyers are not interested in *possible* explanations of events that meet some arbitrary test of rational consistency. Lawyers are interested in the most *probable* explanation of events. Thus lawyers recognize that issues of fact *never* rise to the level of 100 percent or absolute certainty. As the analytical philosophers of our own century have shown, only in matters of pure logic or pure mathematics can one attain such certainty in any event, and that is only because such certainty is built into the system from the start. Even philosophers like Stephen Toulmin of the University of Leeds are advocating the use of evidential models such as those found in the law to advance their efforts at probing more deeply into the nature of the universe.[8] For example, Mortimer Adler[9] concludes his presentation of the traditional proofs of God's existence with an appeal to the legal standards of proof—namely the "preponderance of evidence" standard in civil cases and the proof-beyond-a-reasonable-doubt standard applied in criminal cases:

> If I am able to say no more than that a preponderance of reasons favor believing that God exists, I can still say I have advanced reasonable grounds for that belief. . . . I am persuaded that God exists, either beyond a reasonable doubt or by a preponderance of reasons in favor of that conclusion over reasons against it. I am, therefore, willing to terminate this inquiry with

the statement that I have reasonable grounds for affirming God's existence.[10]

It is critical, therefore, for the Christian apologist to remember, at the outset of the apologetical task, two critical points: (1) The burden of proof for establishing the claims of Christianity concerning the person and work of Christ are on the Christian, since he is the one asserting an affirmative case for Christ. (2) The unbeliever must never be allowed to require a level of proof for matters of fact that in principle are not possible to establish, since matters of fact always involve issues of probability. However, regardless of whether the civil or criminal standard is applied,[11] we will establish that the case for the central claims of Christianity are able to be established "beyond a reasonable doubt and to a moral certainty."

7

A Lawyer's Case
for Christianity
An Apologetic for the Tough-Minded

In the next chapters, we will approach the case for Christianity by addressing four questions: (1) How good are the primary source documents (the Gospels of Matthew, Mark, Luke and John) that contain the claims of Jesus Christ? (2) How reliable is the testimony contained in those documents about the person of Jesus Christ and particularly His resurrection? (3) Does the resurrection of Jesus Christ establish His deity, or is it just another miracle? (4) If questions 1–3 are resolved by the evidence in favor of Jesus Christ and His claims, what does Jesus Christ have to say about the nature and character of the Bible?

The New Testament Gospel Documents: Factual, Fictional, or Forged?

Any inquiry as to the reliability of the New Testament documents strikes the religious liberal as misguided from the outset. The liberal will argue that the fundamental principles of Christianity are set forth in the Sermon on the Mount and their validity is not affected by the reliability or nonreliability of the framework in which they are found; the important thing is Christ's teachings and His life and deeds. This argument points to the fact that the teachings of Confucius and Plato exist on their own merits regardless of whether they actually existed or not.

While this objection has an initially facile appeal, it cannot be supported by any type of serious analysis of the New Testament record itself. Christianity at its heart is not a set of moral teachings or ethics—it is Good News. It is the story of the redemption of man by God who became man. Take away Christ from Christianity and you are not left with moral teachings—you are left with an immoral religion built on the false promises of a deluded and defrauding megalomaniac. All four of the Gospels center around the last week of the life of Christ, thus giving emphasis to the centrality of His death for the sins of humankind. In fact, the old Lutheran dogmaticians called Christ's preaching of the Law his "alien work" to make clear that a ministry of wrath and condemnation was *not* why the Son of Man came into the world.[1] The Law does not distinguish Christianity from any other religions, as C. S. Lewis makes clear in *The Abolition of Man*.

But isn't all this talk of what Christ said in the Gospels actually getting the theological horse before the logical cart? Surely everyone knows that "experts" have shown that the New Testament Gospels contain all kinds of unreliable stories written hundreds of years after the events they record by inebriated monks (or worse, perverted monks of the type depicted in the film version of Umberto Eco's book *The Name of the Rose*) who were trying to establish the authority of the Catholic church over the ignorant masses. These fish stories grew over time until somebody hit upon the resurrection as the ultimate story of this mythical Jesus Christ who evolved out of oral tradition in Palestine. Professor Avrum Stroll, in a lecture to a philosophy club at the University of British Columbia, summarized this view aptly:

"An accretion of legends grew up about this figure Jesus, was incorporated into the gospels by various devotees of the movement, was rapidly spread throughout the Mediterranean world by the ministry of St. Paul; and because this is so, it is impossible to separate these legendary elements in the purported descriptions of Jesus from those which in fact were true of him."[2]

Unfortunately, Dr. Stroll has committed the unpardonable sin of the historian—instead of using the primary source materials (of which, as we shall shortly discover, the New Testament Gospels themselves are a singularly magnificent example), Stroll instead relies upon modern authorities to cast doubt upon the documents themselves. As C. S. Lewis pointed out, however, this is decidedly *not* scholarship and ends up appealing to what twentieth-century man *wishes* first-century man had said. Lewis parallels modern biblical critics with literary critics who have attempted to get at the true sources of Lewis's own work The Chronicles of Narnia. Though the argument was entirely logical, Lewis found that the results were never *once* correct![3] Historians who attempt to weave a picture of Jesus Christ and yet do not consider the primary source documents from which we derive our knowledge of Christ will be engaged in either autobiography or philosophy. They will not be doing history.

THE NEW TESTAMENT GOSPELS AND THE STRENGTH OF THE DOCUMENTARY TRAIL: THE GOSPELS VS. THE GALLIC WARS

But, the critic responds, there was surely both time and motivation for the New Testament writers to embellish the Gospel accounts. With respect to the issue of the time interval, even liberal scholars of the New Testament have been forced to admit that the earliest documents date close to the events they record. For example, Bishop James A. T. Robinson has concluded that all four of the New Testament Gospels were written before A.D. 70, a date even earlier than what most conservative scholars have claimed.[4] Robinson's conclusions are by no means out of the mainstream of biblical scholarship. William F. Albright, considered the Dean of American Archaeologists, put it this way: "We can already say emphatically that there is no longer any solid basis for dating any book of the New Testament after about A.D. 80, two full generations before the date between 130 and 150 given by the more radical New Testament critics of today."[5]

As for the time interval between the events and the original recordation of those events, it is instructive to compare the case for the New Testament Gospels with other works of antiquity. The Gospels not only come sooner upon the events they record but the number of manuscript copies far outnumber that of any other work of the ancient world. For example, Caesar's *Gallic Wars* (written in 58–50 B.C.) survive today on the basis of approximately 10 manuscripts, the oldest of which is dated about 900 years after the events. Thucydides' *History* (c. 460–400 B.C.) as well as the Herodotus's *History* (c. 480–425 B.C.) are known to us through eight manuscripts, the earliest of which is dated c. A.D. 900. The poems of the Roman playwright Catullus (c. 84–54 B.C.) are known to us from just three manuscripts, the earliest of which dates from the late fourteenth century. F. F. Bruce, former Rylands Professor of Biblical Criticism and Exegesis at the University of Manchester, concludes that, "no classical scholar would listen to an argument that the authenticity of Herodotus or Thucydides is in doubt because the earliest MSS of their works which are of any use to us are over 1,300 years later than the originals."[6]

Sir Frederick G. Kenyon, formerly director and principal librarian of the British Museum, puts the evidence for the reliability and integrity of the New Testament Gospels in the following historical perspective:

> In no other case is the interval of time between the composition of the book and the date of the earliest extant manuscript so short as in that of the New Testament. The books of the New Testament were written in the latter part of the first century; the earliest extant manuscripts (trifling scraps excepted)

are of the fourth century—say, from 250 to 300 years later. This may sound a considerable interval, but it is nothing to that which parts most of the great classical authors from their earliest manuscripts. We believe that we have in all essentials an accurate text of the seven extant plays of Sophocles; yet the earliest substantial manuscript upon which it is based was written more than 1,400 years after the poet's death. Aeschylus, Aristophanes, and Thucydides are in the same state; while with Euripides the interval is increased to 1,600 years. For Plato it may be put at 1,300 years, for Demosthenes as low as 1,200.[7]

The 250- to 300-year gap of which Kenyon refers has, since that time, been substantially filled in with numerous papyri portions of the New Testament documents. This led Kenyon, before his death, to conclude that "[t]he interval, then, between the dates of original composition and the earliest extant evidence becomes so small as to be in fact negligible, and the last foundation for any doubt that the Scriptures have come down to us substantially as they were written has now been removed. Both the *authenticity* and the *general integrity* of the books of the New Testament may be regarded as finally established."[8]

In short, from a lawyer's viewpoint these documents are in solid shape and would surely, as Simon Greenleaf argued, be admissible under the so-called "ancient documents" exception to the hearsay rule.[9] They give no evidence of tampering, are well-attested as coming from a strong tradition of manuscript evidence, arise almost on top of the events they record, and have no peer among all works of antiquity based on the sheer number of excellent and early manuscript copies. The documents are reliable historically, applying the commonly accepted canons of historical scholarship used to determine if any work that predates the printing press has reached us in substantially the same shape in which it was authored.

Finally, the argument that the Gospel records were somehow doctored or faked hundreds of years after the events they record (the position offered without any credible evidence to substantiate it by, among others, Professor Hugh Trevor-Roper of Oxford), is dealt with by Lord Chancellor Hailsham, England's highest-ranking legal scholar:

> [What] renders the argument invalid is a fact about fakes of all kinds which I learned myself in the course of a case I did in which there was in question the authenticity of a painting purporting to be by, and to be signed by, Modigliani. This painting, as the result of my Advice on Evidence, was shown to be a fake by X-ray evidence. But in the course of my researches I was supplied by my instructing solicitor with a considerable bibliography concerning the nature of fakes of all kinds and how to detect them. There was one point made by the author of one of these books which is of direct relevance to the point I am discussing. Although fakes can often be made which confuse or actually deceive contemporaries of the faker, the experts, or even the not-so-expert, of a later age can invariably detect them, whether fraudulent or not, because the faker cannot fail to include stylistic or other material not obvious to contemporaries because they are contemporaries, but which stand out a mile to later observers because they reflect the standards, or the materials, or the styles of a succeeding age to that of the author whose work is being faked.[10]

The conclusion is inescapable: The New Testament Gospel records have been transmitted to us in substantially the same condition in which they were composed.[11] They more than fulfill the evidential test for *transmissional reliability.*

MATTHEW, MARK, LUKE, AND JOHN IN THE DOCK

But the skeptic raises another issue at the point that the reliability of the New Testament Gospels is established. Even if their reliability is conceded, how good is the testimony it records? Just because the documents have come down to us in reliable fashion does not, *ipso facto,* mean that the statements recorded in those documents are true and accurate.

This is particularly important since the apostolic writers make plain that Jesus Christ claimed to be no less than God in the flesh come to earth to save sinful man by dying an atoning death on the cross.[12] These same witnesses then go on to record that crucifixion in agonizing detail and then assert a literal physical resurrection from the dead. The efforts of liberal theologians to make Jesus Christ into a pale Galilean moralist who preached pacifism tell us much about the interpreters but this picture is utterly foreign to the historical figure of the primary source documents.

Here the law can again assist us in determining whether the New Testament testimony to Jesus Christ can be impeached and found unreliable or whether it stands the test of rigorous cross-examination.

First, it must be remembered that testimony is generally presumed to be truthful unless impeached or otherwise successfully attacked on cross-examination. This is consistent with ordinary life, where we operate as if people are telling us the truth unless the evidence indicates otherwise. Those who go through life assuming everyone is always lying are called paranoiacs. Therefore we note at the outset that the burden of proof for establishing the unreliability of the Gospel witnesses is on the skeptic. Can he meet his burden of proof?

At this point it is useful to employ a construct for uncovering perjury that has been called "the finest work on that subject."[13] A fourfold test for the exposing of perjury has been developed by McCloskey and Schoenberg. That test involves the following factors: "*internal* and *external* defects in the *witness himself* on the one hand and in the *testimony itself* on the other."[14] The diagram of the construct is on the following page: (Diagram is from p. 141 of Montgomery's *Human Rights and Human Dignity.*)

The issue of *internal defects* refers to whether the New Testament Gospel writers suffered from defects in character that cast doubts on the veracity of their work. Do they display a propensity to "bend the truth" to their own designs with an eye to presenting themselves or their pet cause in the most favorable light? Do the witnesses have past convictions for fraud, which under legal rules

A Construct for Exposing Perjury

INTERNAL DEFECTS

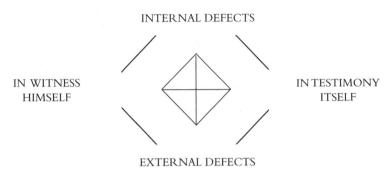

IN WITNESS
HIMSELF

IN TESTIMONY
ITSELF

EXTERNAL DEFECTS

of evidence are always admissible to impeach a witness when the issue of that witness's truthfulness is at issue?

The Gospel writers, however, are the antithesis of clever schemers. They are direct and plain about their own faults and go to seemingly great pains to establish that they are presenting facts and not fables. The apostle Peter puts it clearly: "We did not follow cleverly invented stories (Greek *Mythoi*: *myths*) when we told you about the power and coming of our Lord Jesus Christ, but we were eyewitnesses of His majesty (2 Peter 1:16).

Luke explicitly relies on the "many infallible proofs" of Christ's resurrection appearances. The apostle Paul urges Procurator Festus to check out his claims about Christ for himself since Paul is so confident that a factual investigation of his message concerning Christ will vindicate the case for Christianity.[15] Paul's method is instructive—he did the work of an apologist and left the results to God.

But didn't the evangelists have a motive to lie in order to achieve increased prestige in the eyes of the nascent Christian community or to enhance their economic standing among the Jews or the Romans? This argument, unfortunately, is not tenable. Those who testified of Christ before the bar of public opinion in first-century Palestine uniformly lost all earthly wealth and prestige they might otherwise have enjoyed. This point is made with great precision and power by the fourth-century church historian

Eusebius of Caesarea and by Hugo Grotius, the great Dutch legal scholar and Christian apologist.[16]

In fact, the authors of the New Testament Gospels had every motive to get the story of Jesus Christ *utterly accurate* in light of their martyrdom, which occurred precisely because of what they wrote and taught concerning Jesus. If the disciples put their pens to paper in order to line their financial pocket, the effort was a total failure. There is no historical record of *any* of the Twelve dying with wealth. Rather the records indicate they went about distributing wealth to the poor and preaching against the mindless accumulation of possessions. Besides, this would have been in direct contradiction of their Lord's specific teachings concerning lying and the vanity of living solely to acquire wealth.[17]

But what about the *testimony itself?* Perhaps it is internally inconsistent or self-contradictory. The Gospel records do not give four identical accounts of the events they record. Does this not show inconsistency and offer proof that the witnesses are fabricating their testimony or are engaged in collusion?

In fact, the presence of four different *but not inconsistent* versions of events is one of the strongest evidentiary factors in favor of the integrity of the Gospel writers. Identical statements by witnesses is one of the surest signs of collusion.[18] When preparing a case for trial, a lawyer assumes that they will be prevented by the judge from wasting the jury's time by presenting multiple witnesses whose testimony in substance is exactly the same. It is only because different witnesses have additional perspectives and evidence to offer that the advocate is allowed to present "cumulative" testimony. Thus, for example, at trial a lawyer will likely not be allowed to offer four witnesses to testify that the traffic light was red. However, if one witness testifies as to road conditions on the day in question, one as to the speed of the plaintiff's vehicle, one as to the speed of the defendant's vehicle, and one as to whether a pedestrian was in the crosswalk or not, it is likely that the court will allow all four to testify even if they each also testify that the light was red.

The fact is, with respect to the Gospel accounts, no single author claims to give the definitive treatment of the life of Jesus. In fact, the writers themselves specifically disclaim any claim to an exhaustive record of the life and ministry of Christ (John 20:30–31; John 21:25). We should not be surprised if Jesus spoke the same words more than once (i.e., same message to different groups) or that He threw the moneychangers out of the temple twice. As Montgomery puts it: "And suppose He did throw the moneychangers out of the temple twice: is it not strange, in light of their activity and His principles, that He *only* threw them out twice? (We would have expected it every Saturday—Sabbath—night.)"[19] If the New Testament Gospel writers intended to present themselves and their integrity and intelligence to the world, they failed miserably. Instead, they present themselves and others in the apostolic band as regularly in need of correction and rebuke by Christ and by each other. At one point Jesus brutally analyzes their condition saying of them that they are "slow of heart to believe all that the prophets have spoken" (Luke 24:25).

But what about external defects in the actual testimony itself? Doesn't archaeology or other extrabiblical scholarship disprove the veracity of the biblical writers?

It should be noted initially that the careful observer of the New Testament Gospels is immediately struck by the manner in which the writers, rather than speaking in platitudes that cannot ever be checked out because they lack any historical referent, instead impregnate their writing with repeated, and detailed, historical references. The Gospels, rather than starting out with indications that they are divorced from history (e.g., the once-upon-a-time approach so typical of fairytales and much mythic and pagan sacred literature), begin with "Caesar Augustus issued a decree that a census should be taken" (Luke 2:1). The following passage from Luke is typical: "In the fifteenth year of the reign of Tiberius Caesar—when Pontius Pilate was governor of Judea, Herod tetrarch of Galilee, his brother Philip tetrarch of Iturea and Traconitis, and

Lysanias tetrarch of Abilene—during the priesthood of Annas and Caiaphas, the word of God came to John son of Zechariah in the desert. He went into all the country around the Jordan, preaching a baptism of repentance for the forgiveness of sins" (Luke 3:1–3).

As for the discoveries of archaeology, they have consistently supported the biblical accounts. In fact, archaeology has been the best friend Christianity could hope to have, and its results repeatedly are found to vindicate New Testament geography, chronology, and history. From the discovery of the Jubililees-Qumran Calendar by the French Dead Sea scholar Jaubert (which harmonized the long-held supposed contradiction in the Gospels as to the day of Christ's crucifixion), to the discovery in 1961 of the famous "Pilate inscription" (establishing what critics had said never existed—a pagan reference to Pontius Pilate), the New Testament Gospel writers' integrity has repeatedly been tested and found trustworthy.[20]

SUCCESSFUL LYING IS A FULL-TIME OCCUPATION

There is a widely held perception among nonlawyers that deception or lying is fairly easy to get away with in society and in a court of law. While this appears to be the case when the lie involves matters of relative unimportance or is an isolated fact, in reality the effort and intelligence necessary to successfully lie in a court of law is simply staggering. Richard Givens, in his standard text on trial advocacy, has described in detail the tortuous labyrinth that the deceptive witness must embark upon, all the while under the relentless pursuit of the cross-examiner. Givens has provided a diagram showing the contrast between the mental gymnastics that the lying witness must engage in as compared to someone who is simply telling the truth. The following chart shows the direct and uncomplicated analysis that the truthful witness engages in to tell his story.

Note that he must recollect the event and then select what portion of the event he is going to testify to. The truthful witness then selects the symbols by which he will communicate (words, ges-

The Mental Process in "simple"
—i.e. truthful—communication

Event

Recollection

Portion selected to be communicated

Symbols

Interpretation by listener

The Lying Witness

Event

Original recollection

Distorton to serve purpose
of witness

Comparison with belief or knowledge of examiner	Comparison with prior statements of witnesses	Comparison for obvious, provable discrepancies

Estimate chance
of discovery

Decision to continue with
or revise original story

Selection of intended
communication

Symbols

Interpretation by listener

tures, screams, voice inflection, etc.). Finally, the truthteller must keep in mind how his communication will be interpreted so that he is careful to use communicative symbols that speak truthfully to the listener.

Contrast the relative simplicity of telling the truth with Givens's diagrammatic presentation of the various balls that must be juggled by the deceptive witness. Notice how the liar has at least three balls that must be juggled simultaneously, all the while analyzing his chances of being discovered: first, he must be assured he says nothing that he knows or thinks contradicts what his cross-examiner knows (or what he thinks his examiner knows); second, he needs to be consistent in his lie—it cannot be changed ("liars must have good memories"); and third, he must be certain that his lie cannot be contradicted by external data. Givens concludes that the art of prolonged deception by a witness requires a Herculean intellectual effort, creating such psychological strain that few can withstand it:

> If one is lying or strongly biased, it is not enough to simply dredge up whatever mental trace there may be of the event and attempt to articulate it in answer to a question. Instead, all of the various elements mentioned must be weighed, a decision made as to the best approach, a reply contrived that is expected to be most convincing, and then an effort made to launch this communication into the minds of the audience. *The person with a wide angle of divergence between what is recalled and the impression sought to be given is thus at an almost helpless disadvantage, especially if confronting a cross-examiner who understands the predicament.*[21]

Now let us assume for the sake of argument that Matthew, Mark, Luke, and John were the personality types who wanted to perpetrate a widespread deception. We will set aside for the moment what we have already seen—that their personalities, and the message they proclaimed, were particularly ill-suited to such deception. Added to this fact is the reality that this would also have to be a conspiracy and not just a matter of one witness calculating the implications of their singular deception. Could they have pulled off such a deception even if they had wanted to?

While the witnesses to Christ's life, death, and resurrection were not subject to being put on a formal witness stand in a court of law and subject to cross-examination, other factors converge to operate as *de facto* cross-examination. Most important, the Gospel writers and witnesses made it their practice to present the case for Jesus Christ initially within the context of the Jewish synagogue—thus effectively subjecting their testimony to the rigorous rebuttal of the hostile religious community who had an intimate knowledge of the Old Testament and surely would not have stood idly by while the Gospel witnesses falsely claimed that Jesus had fulfilled numerous prophecies. Those religious leaders had, as Simon Greenleaf puts it, the "means, motive and opportunity" to decimate the apostolic witnesses if indeed they could.[22] In addition, the Romans surely would have produced the body of Christ if it existed if for no other reason than to restore their treasured order. F. F. Bruce summarizes this point as follows:

> It was not only friendly eyewitnesses that the early preachers had to reckon with; there were others less well disposed who were also conversant with the main facts of the ministry and death of Jesus. The disciples could not afford to risk inaccuracies (not to speak of willful manipulation of the facts), which would at once be exposed by those who would be only too glad to do so. On the contrary, one of the strong points in the original apostolic preaching is the confident appeal to the knowledge of the hearers; they not only said, "We are witnesses of these things," but also, "As you yourselves also know" (Acts 2:22). Had there been any tendency to depart from the facts in any material respect, the possible presence of hostile witnesses in the audience would have served as a further corrective.[23]

We may confidently conclude that the Gospel writers withstand the most rigorous cross-examination, not only as to their character but also as to the content of their testimony.

8

LAWYERS AND RESURRECTIONS

We must make deductions on the basis of sound evidence, even when conclusions are astonishing. As Sherlock Holmes—a man who always relied on evidence—said to Watson, "When you have eliminated the impossible, whatever remains, *however improbable,* must be the truth."[1] Holmes advises that facts must always be allowed to adjust theories. When applied to the resurrection, the investigator will not rule out a resurrection *a priori* but will first investigate the data.

The resurrection is presented by the apostolic band as the heart of their entire case. The apostle Paul is so bold as to hinge the case for Christianity explicitly, and entirely, on the facticity of the resurrection. Jesus Himself pinned all His claims on the factual verification that His resurrection would provide.[2] But did the resurrection, as a matter of fact, actually occur in a way that can be verified?

First, we must deal with the objection that a resurrection is a supernatural miracle that has been shown to be both philosophically impossible (by virtue of the arguments of the Scottish philosopher David Hume) and scientifically impossible (by Einsteinian physics).

As for Hume's argument against the miraculous, C. S. Lewis has shown that Hume believed he could eliminate the need to investigate the factual case for the resurrection by postulating a philosophical argument against the miraculous. Hume reasoned from the initial premise (totally unsupportable, we might add, especially in an Einsteinian universe) that "a firm and unalterable experience has established the laws of nature." Lewis shows that this led Hume to the totally circular conclusion that "[t]here must be a uniform experience against every miraculous event" and "that a dead man should come to life has never been observed in any age or country."[3] As Montgomery has pointed out, there is no way of determining *a priori* whether a resurrection has occurred unless one first checks out the evidence.[4] Hume allowed rationalistic eighteenth-century man to sit back in his easy chair and ignore the evidence for the resurrection without so much as lifting a finger to investigate the claim inductively. Contra Holmes, Hume and his followers do not even have to check out evidence because their supposed knowledge of the nature of the universe makes it unnecessary.

As for the argument that an Einsteinian universe has negated the need to check out events that violate "natural law," the case is actually exactly the opposite. "Natural law" theories have been shown to be more a reflection of eighteenth-century man's religious commitment to logical consistency and deductive systems of order than it was the result of an inductive study of the universe that was willing to let data reign regardless of the metaphysical consequences.[5] The fact is that no one has a pipeline into the ultimate nature of the universe such that he knows, without checking out the evidence, what is "reasonable" in terms of events. A resurrection may not have occurred since that day in first-century Palestine, but the fact that it has not been repeated has no bearing on whether it *in fact* took place once in history. A resurrection is an historical claim and it must be investigated inductively and not dismissed on the basis of a thoroughly discredited method of philosophical reasoning based on a basic arrogance that one knows what is "reasonable" without checking out the evidence.

The issue of the missing body is one of great force. The empty tomb itself has been sufficient on its own merits to bring skeptics to Christian faith. For example, attorney Frank Morrison converted to Christianity on the sole basis of his investigation of the factual case for the resurrection. Morrison's argument is that if Jesus did not rise from the dead, then there are only three interest groups who might have had a motivation to remove the body: the Romans, the Jewish religious leaders, and the disciples. The Romans craved peace and order so that they might extract taxes from the Jews. The last thing they wanted was controversy. Morrison notes that the Jews had every motivation to preserve their religious influence and control, while the disciples would hardly steal the body and then go out and die for what they knew was a lie.[6]

But, the skeptic responds, works such as Schonfield's *Passover Plot* and Von Daniken's *Chariot of the Gods* have surely established alternative explanations of the resurrection story. Since the reader has already seen the application of the legal principles of the "burden of proof" and "probabilistic reasoning," there should be little difficulty applying these rules to such alternative explanations. Schonfield argues that Jesus, Joseph of Arimathea, and Lazarus were coconspirators who agreed that Jesus would orchestrate His own crucifixion, pass out on the cross—thus fooling the Roman guards that He was dead, and then revive in the cool confines of the tomb. Jesus then indeed did miraculously revive and fool the disciples into thinking He was resurrected.[7] Note that this position does not answer the question as to what ultimately happened to the body, nor does it answer how this squares with Christ's own teachings about honesty and truthtelling. Von Daniken's theory is that Jesus was the cosmic equivalent of a Martian who had otherworldly powers whereby He appeared to have resurrected.

What can be said about such mere *possibilities?* Even though Von Daniken himself would be subject to character impeachment based on his convictions for embezzlement, fraud, and forgery in

Switzerland,[8] we need not go that far. These theories are based on mere possibilities. But as Montgomery has written, virtually anything is possible, but courts are interested in probabilities based on evidence and not theories based on mere speculation.[9]

Finally, a word must be said about the objection to the resurrection posed by atheistic philosopher Anthony Flew. Flew says Christians simply prefer a biological miracle (i.e., Christ's resurrection from the dead) to a psychological miracle (i.e., the disciples dying for what they knew to be false). But as we have seen, the issue is not what "preference" a person has for the evidence. The question is what interpretation of the evidence considers the maximum amount of factual data. If the eyewitness accounts have Jesus dead at point A and then alive at point B, you have a resurrection. It does nothing to ignore evidence on the basis of self-created "preferences." The "deluded disciples" argument is simply untenable under the canons of evidence employed in a court of law. There are simply too many facts that refute the position.[10]

Thomas Sherlock, master of the Temple Church and Bishop of London, answered the question in the eighteenth century as to how much evidence was required to prove a factual resurrection:

> Suppose you saw a Man publickly executed, his Body afterwards wounded by the Executioner, and carry'd and laid in the Grave; that after this you shou'd be told, that the Man was come to Life again: What wou'd you suspect in this Case? Not that the Man had never been dead; for that you saw your self: But you wou'd suspect whether he was now alive. But wou'd you say, this Case excluded all human Testimony; and that Men could not possibly discern, whether one with whom they convers'd familiarly, was alive or no? Upon what Ground cou'd you say this? A Man rising from the Grave is an Object of Sense, and can give the same Evidence of his being alive, as any other Man in the World can give. So that a Resurrection consider'd only as a Fact to be proved by Evidence, is a plain Case; it requires no greater Ability in the Witnesses, than that they be able to distinguish between a Man dead, and a Man alive: A

Point, in which I believe every Man living thinks himself a
Judge.[11]

IS THE RESURRECTION JUST ANOTHER MIRACLE?

But the critic responds, isn't the resurrection just another miracle (like the "healings" performed by the televangelist)? As the
existentialist philosophers and analytical psychologists have been
quick to point out, death is the ultimate leveler of us all. Carl Gustav Jung and Mircea Eliade found that images associated with
death are cross-cultural and indeed are "archetypes" of the collective unconscious. We all fear death in some sense, and the funeral is
an ancient effort to help the surviving community come to grips
with the devastation and seeming irrationality of death.[12]

Our point? If God was indeed to become man and give us
insight into one issue, it would be on the enigma of death. In Jesus
Christ we find the announcement that we have brought about our
own doom by our cosmic rebellion against God, but that God has
acted to deal with the separation created by man when man was
wholly incapable of effecting such a reconciliation. Jesus claimed to
come to earth to deal with man's sin ("For the Son of Man came
to seek and to save what was lost" [Luke 19:10]) and to give a final
answer to death for all who will believe. If ever there was a basis for
worship, it is here. Instead of coming to earth to engage in trivia
(curing hangnails, for example, or presenting weight-loss programs), the eternal Logos became fully human in the womb of the
virgin to achieve a rescue that only God could effect.

Finally, if we are presented with a choice as to whose testimony
as to the meaning of the resurrection is most competent—Jesus' or
that of the twentieth-century critics—we suggest it is infinitely
more reasonable to accept the testimony of the One who actually
accomplished His resurrection. If you ask Jesus what the proper
interpretation of His resurrection is, He confidently answers that it
establishes His diety.[13] Until the critics accomplish a resurrection,

the testimony of the One who actually resurrected is the best evidence.

Jesus' Testimony about the Nature, Character, and Reliability of the Scriptures

If, as we have argued, Christ's resurrection establishes His deity, then we should be quick to hear Him if He has pronounced on any topic, including the reliability of the Scriptures. On this topic Christ could not have been clearer. As for the Old Testament, He unambiguously testifies that it is accurate to the smallest jot and tittle, while He guarantees that the coming New Testament will be guarded in its transmission by the Holy Spirit through the pens of the eyewitnesses to His resurrection—namely the apostolic band.[14]

If one takes a critical view of Scripture, it will ultimately, if one is logical and consistent, swallow up even the Gospel itself. The history of biblical criticism is solid evidence of this point. The Historical-Critical School began "innocently" in the eighteenth century with the French physician Jean Astruc and his questioning of the Mosaic authorship of the Pentateuch, spread quickly to the application of source criticism to major prophets like Isaiah and speculations about multiple authors, and finally collapsed in the twentieth century with Rudolf Bultmann and the later Death-of-God school, which ended in total skepticism over the historical Christ, and therefore, the historical Gospel itself.[15]

Notice that we have assiduously avoided engaging in circular reasoning. We have not started out assuming that the New Testament Gospels are the Word of God and then finding that they present Christ as claiming to be God and verifying His claim by His resurrection. Instead, we have built the case inductively, allowing the final verification of the claims of Christ by way of His resurrection to rest solidly on the reliability of the documentary evidence. The case builds inductively to the final conclusion of the total reliability and inerrancy of the Scriptures *not* because we have assumed that axiom into the argument at the outset but because we discover it at the end of our evidential inquiry. In short, we follow a basic principle of all investigation in the factual world and one laid out precisely by Sherlock Holmes: "I have no data yet. It is a capital mistake to theorize before one has data. Insensibly one begins to twist facts to suit theories, instead of theories to suit facts."[16]

Is the factual case for Christianity one hundred percent certain?[17] We have already seen how this cannot in principle be the required standard to prove any issue of fact. We operate in everyday life on the basis of probabilistic reasoning, applying this method in both the realm of the mundane (eating the strawberry on the fork rather than the fork) to the most serious verdicts a society can render (sentence of death given even though the jury is instructed that the evidence need not reach absolute certainty). But can we base ultimate concerns (Jesus' death, resurrection, deity, and claim to be the sole entrance gate to heaven) on such probabilistic reasoning? As the analytical philosophers have shown, we have no other choice. Only propositions of pure mathematics or deductive logic are capable of being demonstrated absolutely, but they do not deal with issues of fact. All assertions of fact (what the analytical philosophers call "synthetic assertions") are by their very nature limited to probabilistic confirmation.

SUMMATION: SOME FREE LEGAL ADVICE

The evidence for the central claim of Christianity—that God was "in Christ reconciling the world unto Himself"—is overwhelmingly solid. We have seen that the evidences (documents and witnesses) are the type that are offered and admitted in courts of law routinely. The eternal consequences of this evidence are staggering. The evidence itself must be investigated on its own merits. The evidence, if fairly considered, leads the skeptic to an inevitable verdict: the truth claims of Christianity are valid. One may resist and turn away from the consequences of the admissible evidence on behalf of Christian faith, but that is an altogether different issue from claiming that the evidence itself is insufficient to compel belief. Simon Greenleaf has summed up the case well:

> All that Christianity asks of men on this subject, is, that they would be consistent with themselves; that they would treat its evidences as they treat the evidence of other things; and that they would try and judge its actors and witnesses, as they deal with their fellow men, when testifying to human affairs and actions, in human tribunals. Let the witnesses be compared with themselves, with each other, and with surrounding facts and circumstances; and let their testimony be sifted, as it were given in a court of justice, on the side of the adverse party, the witness being subjected to rigorous cross-examination. The result, it is confidently believed, will be an undoubting conviction of their integrity, ability, and truth. In the course of such an examination, the undesigned coincidences will multiply upon us at every step in our progress; the probability of the veracity of the witnesses and of the reality of the occurrences which they related will increase, until it acquires, for all practical purposes, the value and force of demonstration.[18]

While the use of the law is helpful in determining the facts of the Christian faith, can it help in the proper interpretation of those facts? Critics argue that the interpretation of facts is in the realm of the subjective, since all interpretations are ultimately a matter of personal preference. The result of this wholesale subjectivity with respect to the historian's task is that, as Professor Keith Windschuttle points out, "the central point upon which history was founded no longer holds: there is no fundamental distinction anymore between history and myth."[19]

To the contrary, however, the law not only can help us to sift the evidence offered on behalf of Christian truth claims, it can also provide us the tools to properly interpret that evidence. Indeed, the utter chaos in theology today is not so much a matter of confessional differences as it is hermeneutical perspectives. As Montgomery puts it: "On the one side, regardless of denominational commitment, are those who insist on interpreting the biblical text in its natural (not necessarily literal) sense; on the other, those who flatly deny that any such objective interpretation is possible and who therefore see the text as a reflection of its original environment and in dialectic interaction with the contemporary interpreter. It may almost be reduced to: Billy Graham ("The Bible says") vs. Robert Funk's Jesus Seminar."[20]

The law can provide necessary clarity on the issue of the proper interpretation of the Gospels. In general, the law adopts the practice of traditional orthodox historical theology in interpreting a document in its "historical-grammatical" context. The approach of theology is well summarized by Professor Eugene F. A. Klug as the fundamental principle "that there is one intended, literal, proper sense to any given passage in Scripture *(sensus literalis unus est); also* that the Scripture is its own best interpreter *(Scriptura Scripturam interpretat* or *Scriptura sui ipsius interpres). . . .* The literal sense thus always stands first, and each interpreter must guard against cluttering that which is being communicated with his own ideas, lest the meaning be lost."[21]

The historical-grammatical approach to Scripture is soundly supported by the law.[22] In short, legal principles of document interpretation would vindicate the traditional interpretation of the New Testament Gospels and utterly vindicate its interpretation confirmed by the overwhelming consensus of the Christian church for more than 2,000 years and reflected in the ecumenical creeds—namely, that the Christ of the Gospels is truly a historical figure who claimed to be God in the flesh and vindicated His claims by living a perfect life and dying an atoning death for the sins of the world, ultimately verifying those claims by His physical resurrection from the dead. Efforts to introduce a later contradictory oral tradition (which, as Luther pointed out, was the approach of Rome in his day, and is today the approach of the Jesus Seminar) would be immediately rejected in a court of law by the "parole evidence rule." In fact, later oral tradition that contradicts the written text is not even allowed to be presented to the jury. As a matter of law, the judge can and will rule that the oral contradictory statements of a supposed later tradition are inadmissible.[23]

Thus the legal approach to the biblical Gospel not only vindicates the case for Christ—it also vindicates the traditional "natural sense" interpretation of those Gospels that reveals the redemptive life, death, and resurrection of Jesus Christ confessed by the three ecumenical creeds of Christendom held to by all Christians—Orthodox, Catholic, and Protestant—for two millennia.

9

A LAWYER AMONG THE ARTISTS
AN APOLOGETIC FOR THE TENDER-MINDED

To this point we have concentrated on an objective apologetic, focusing on the tools of historical investigation and the unique insights of legal or juridical apologetics. Since apostolic times, the use of miracle and prophecy have been employed to present the facticity of the Christian Gospel. The objective approach has the benefit of being a public apologetic, open to analysis by all and subject to the twin tenets of analytical philosophy—verification and falsification. But there is a subjective apologetic that must also be considered.

For good reason, Christian apologists have avoided purely subjective appeals to the faith, rightly worried that they can lead to a liberal dilution of the Gospel with a Milquetoast Jesus created from the psyche and not from the historical record. The history of such subjective theologies as seen in Bultmann and his subsequent school of "demythologizing" is a tragic reminder that the Gospel is quickly undermined when objective referents are jettisoned. However, the fundamentalist's "theology of testimony" falls prey to the

same criticism that it, too, is so wholly subjective that it can be easily explained away. Harvard psychologist William James argued that
Christian conversion was simply one of a host of equally valid and
totally subjective and unverifiable religious experiences available in
the marketplace of the world's religions.[1]

And yet the need for a subjective apologetic remains since
many are not swayed by hard evidence. They have artistic sensibilities that are not moved by what appear to be cold issues of fact.
We are very much convinced that the conserving and essentially
affirmative nature of the Lutheran Reformation and the sacramental focus of all truly Lutheran theology (i.e., the "marriage" of
heaven and earth seen in the incarnation and in the sacraments)
provides an objective grounding for a subjective apologetic and
the rescuing of the arts from pagan reductionism. But the poets of
our own day decry the hyperobjectivity of a depersonalized, com-
puter-driven world where personal contact and the human
dimension are being relegated to the ash heap. Crassness is the
order of the day in communication as this world reaps the harvest
of a practical Marxism—a thin materialism that empties the world
of anything sacred. Traditionally, religion and the arts have always
gone together. Beginning with eighteenth-century Rationalism,
this connection has been rent asunder in modern society. So it is
not surprising today to find that higher-level artists continue to
cry out for mystery, transcendence, and meaning beyond the latest
technological gimmick designed for no purpose other than to
make it possible to access largely trivial data and to make money
anywhere, anytime.

The problem for the Christian apologist operating in this sea
of relativism is apparent: How can the objectivity of a factual and
historic Gospel be presented to a generation that appears to be
fully enmeshed in utter subjectivism? Isn't the Gospel compro-
mised the very moment we would even attempt to present a subjective apologetic for the Gospel?

To this point we have concentrated on an apologetic for what

Herbert Feigel has called the "tough-minded"—those who are appealed to by hard, objective evidences and whose problems with Christianity are intellectual in origin.[2] Since most apologetical approaches developed in Christian history have been empirical in nature (employing prophecy, miracle, historical arguments, and the traditional proofs for the existence of God), the resources for the apologist to the tough-minded are many layered.

But the sensitive Christian apologist recognizes that some unbelievers have subjective objections to Christian claims that are as deeply embedded as any purely intellectual difficulty. We will classify these people as the "tender-minded." You will immediately think of those persons whose sensitivities and ultimate concerns lie in the areas of music, art, literature, and the theater. Does the Christian apologist have any apologetical arrows in his quiver for the higher level tender-minded in addition to the historical and juridical evidences we have presented previously? Just as important, how does the apologist resist falling into subjectivism and all its pitfalls when dealing with the tender-minded when the objective evidences for Christian faith do not strike at the level of the deepest perceived need of the tender-minded? The response of the higher level tender-minded to historical and juridical evidences is often not hostile—the evidences simply appear to bounce off.

But what if fallen man across cultures had retained a recognition that he is fractured internally and separated from his Creator and that he is in need of redemption and a total rescue from the outside? Though man as sinner will have pushed down this recognition from his conscious life, if the situation is as we suggest, then he will have only succeeded in repressing these issues into the region of his psyche and subconscious. Under these circumstances, as Montgomery has noted, "redemptive knowledge would surface not in a direct fashion but by way of symbolic patterns. . . . Jungian analytical psychotherapy has indeed identified such redemptive 'archetypes,' or fundamental and universal symbolic patterns, which appear equally in the physical liturgies of ancient alchemists and in the dreams of contemporary business men."[3] Thus if, for example, writers operating as Christians and with sensitivity to these archetypes could employ such objective archetypal images, the result should be a response by the tender-minded person to the Gospel veiled as it were in such sensitive literature. In short, the tender-minded will respond to the symbolic images used in spite of any conscious objections they might have to the Gospel.

THE INKLINGS AND THE *VIA AFFIRMATA:* A LITERARY APOLOGETIC

Christian apologists addressing the tender-minded have historically employed what Charles Williams calls the *via negativa* or way of negation (neither is this thou). Here the apologist uses the artistic works of the secularist to illustrate the enormity of human depravity and man's recognition of his fallen condition and points out that all secular attempts at salvation are doomed to failure. Thus the apologist will point to works like Albert Camus's *La Peste* (The plague) and *La Chute* (The fall), Samuel Beckett's *En attendant Godot* (Waiting for Godot), Jean-Paul Sartre's *Huis clos* (No exit) and *La Nausee* (Nausea), William Golding's *Lord of the Flies,* and William Faulkner's *The Sound and the Fury* to establish that even the secularist recognizes that man is lost and must have an answer from outside of himself. The *via negativa* is an apologetic based on contrasts.

But what of affirmative artistic efforts to point to the Gospel itself? Do they exist, or does sinful man's condition make them ripe only as a source of abuse and delusion? Can the apologist find positive literary comparisons that point to the Gospel on a second level perhaps even deeper than that of the purely cognitive?

The apologetical employment of what Williams also called the *via affirmata,* or way of affirmation, has enemies on two sides within larger Christendom. First, the fundamentalist sees man's sinful condition as obliterating secular pointers to the Gospel derived outside of Scripture itself. He smells compromise in any effort to draw secular parallels to the Gospel outside of the biblical record. On the other hand is the liberal who finds no reliable basis in Scripture to begin with and whose doctrine of sin is therefore always in flux. He sees parallels and equivalence in everything since all religions are saying the same thing. Thus, Jesus and Gandhi end up standing for the same thing. The Greeks created the myth of Zeus, while the Jews of Palestine created the myth of Jesus.

A group of writers in the twentieth century, however, sought to employ trans- or cross-cultural symbolic or subconscious images (the so-called Jungian "archetypes of the collective unconscious") in their literary works. All also wrote tough-minded apologetical works though none had formal training in theology. They came to be known as "The Inklings" and included authors C. S. Lewis (The Chronicles of Narnia, *Out of the Silent Planet, Perelandra, That Hideous Strength*), J. R. R. Tolkien (The Lord of the Rings), and Charles Williams *(All Hallows' Eve, Descent into Hell, Shadows of Ecstasy, War in Heaven).*[4] These writers produced literary works that, on different levels, connect the reader with fundamental redemptive images that are transcultural.[5] Lewis's allegorical efforts in The Chronicles of Narnia and in his science fiction trilogy, Williams's numinous novels of the supernatural world, as well as Tolkien's deep myth done with incredible genius in The Lord of the Rings trilogy are particularly brilliant examples of an apologetic to the tender-minded. In these works, the authors present the basic images of the Gospel in literary forms. These works are objective apologetical operations functioning on the level of the unconscious as they employ objective psychological forms found in every man regardless of how hardened the intellect may be to the Gospel.

But what if the unbeliever senses the drift of this allegorical, mythical, and fictional literature and then simply argues that the Gospels are just another form of allegory, myth, or fiction? Lewis himself deals with that argument:

> I was by now too experienced in literary criticism to regard
> the Gospels as myths. They had not the mythical taste. And yet
> the very matter which they set down in their artless, historical
> fashion—those narrow, unattractive Jews, too blind to the
> mythical wealth of the Pagan world around them—was pre-
> cisely the matter of the great myths. If ever a myth had become
> fact, had been incarnated, it would be just like this. And noth-
> ing else in all literature was just like this. Myths were like it in
> one way. Histories were like it in another. But nothing was
> simply like it. And no person was like the Person it depicted; as
> real, as recognizable, through all that depth of time, as Plato's
> Socrates or Boswell's Johnson (ten times more so than Ecker-
> mann's Goethe or Lockhart's Scott), yet also numinous, lit by a
> light from beyond the world, a god. But if a god—we are no
> longer polytheists—then not a god, but god. Here and here
> only in all time the myth must have become fact; the Word,
> flesh; God, Man. This is not "a religion," nor "a philosophy." It
> is the summing up and actuality of them all.[6]

Welcoming "Pagan Christs": Turning Myth to Fact

Christians must not shy away from literary or other parallels to
the Gospel story. We tend to think that the Gospel is being diluted
in some way when such parallels are drawn in literature, film, or
art. However, such parallels should be encouraged, and we should
not be surprised to find the most sensitive secular authors and
filmmakers, composers, and artists providing such Gospel motifs
despite even their personal opposition to the Gospel. At the point
that the artist attempts to argue that the Gospel is simply another
fairy tale, myth, or allegory, the Christian apologist must recognize
that a shift has occurred. The objection now being raised belongs
in the realm of the tough-minded and can be dealt with effectively
by the historical and juridical evidences we have marshaled in pre-

vious chapters to show that myth has become fact. Lewis in fact welcomed "Pagan Christs":

> We must not be ashamed of the mythical radiance resting on our theology. We must not be nervous about "parallel" and "Pagan Christs": they *ought* to be there—it would be a stumbling block if they weren't. We must not, in false spirituality, withhold our imaginative welcome. If God chooses to be mythopoeic—and is not the sky itself a myth—shall we refuse to be *mythopathic?* For this is the marriage of heaven and earth: Perfect Myth and Perfect Fact: claiming not only our love and our obedience, but also our wonder and delight, addressed to the savage, the child, and the poet in each one of us no less than to the moralist, the scholar, and the philosopher.[7]

Of course Christians should never allow "Pagan Christs" to stand alone. If we begin with the skeptic at myth, we must lead him to the objective reality behind all deep myth. The Inklings and the literary apologists stand as a footnote to Augustine's axiom found at the beginning of *The Confessions: Fecisti nos ad te et inquietum est cor nostrum, donec requiescat in te* (Thou hast made us for Thyself, and our heart is restless till it rest in Thee). The sensitive unbeliever will find in this literature a door opening to the true Narnia, where Christ our Lord reigns and where every tear is wiped away. He will find, if he investigates his interior life honestly, that a piece is missing. Augustine suggests that this piece is cross-shaped.

J. S. Bach as Apologist: The Fifth Evangelist

I once had the remarkable experience of joining more than 500 secular university students jammed into a concert hall to voluntarily subject themselves to the preaching of the Gospel of Christ. For about 35 minutes both sin and the cross were preached clearly and forcefully. More strangely, the event was not sponsored by any church or Christian organization. There was no sign-up sheet or hard sell at the end. In fact, the preachers of the Gospel in its purity were persons who never gave the slightest indication that they themselves personally believed a word of what they were saying.

The event? A performance of Johann Sebastian Bach's Cantata No. 4, *Christ lag in Todesbanden* (Christ lay in death's strong bands). The sponsor? The Ancient Music Ensemble of the University of California at Santa Barbara. Here, supposedly jaded, secular college students sang the following:

> Christ Jesus lay in death's strong bands
> For our offenses given;
> But now at God's right hand He stands
> And brings us life from heaven.
> Therefore let us joyful be
> And sing to God right thankfully
> Loud songs of alleluia! Alleluia!
>
> It was a strange and dreadful strife
> When life and death contended;
> The victory remained with life,
> The reign of death was ended.
> Holy Scripture plainly says
> That death is swallowed up by death,
> Its sting is lost forever. Alleluia!
>
> Here the true Pascal Lamb we see,
> Whom God so freely gave us;
> He died on the accursed tree—
> So strong His love—to save us.
> See, His blood now marks our door;
> Faith points to it;
> Death passes o'er,
> And Satan cannot harm us. Alleluia!
>
> So let us keep the festival
> To which the Lord invites us;
> Christ is Himself the joy of all,
> The sun that warms and lights us.
> Now His grace to us imparts

Eternal sunshine to our hearts;
The night of sin is ended. Alleluia!

Then let us feast this Easter Day
On Christ, the bread of heaven;
The Word of grace has purged away
The old and evil leaven.
Christ alone our souls will feed;
He is our meat and drink indeed;
Faith lives upon no other! Alleluia![8]

While Bach is not operating in the archetypal world of the Inklings and the literary apologists in precisely the same way, his work is very consciously sacramental in nature—seeking a sacred union of earth and heaven. It is widely argued that Bach is in fact the greatest composer who ever lived, though he never composed a single symphony or opera, as did Mozart.[9] It is not only the beauty of Bach's melodic lines nor the depth and complexity of his music, written for essentially every serious instrument of his day, that sets Bach apart from all musicians. Nor is it the staggering volume of work Bach produced—as of this writing Hanssler of Germany is predicting that the complete set of his works will be comprised of 171 CDs. What sets Bach apart is his seriousness as a theologian and his ability to vertically connect the listener to eternity—so much so that he is often referred to as "The Fifth Evangelist." As Charles Sanford Terry, Gunther Stiller, and others have pointed out, Bach was a student of Scripture and a careful theologian. Jaroslav Pelikan, in fact, has determined that essentially all of Luther's 38 hymns can be reconstructed—both music and text—from the works of Bach alone.[10] As a committed student of the Lutheran Reformation (Robin Leaver says Bach's personal library at his death was of the highest quality and was replete with serious Reformation theology. Nearly all the titles were by Luther or by other orthodox Lutheran theologians), Bach chafed under a Calvinist court prince and yearned for an appointment to a Lutheran church, where full expression to the theology of Luther and the Reformation could have free reign.[11] Thus, Schweitzer argues that "had Luther not been an artist, Bach would never have been able to write his sacred concert-music for church purposes and as part of the church service."[12] Bach was an evangelist. The transcendental nature of the texts he sets to music along with his deeply personal commitment to the saving Gospel dwarf all who might be compared to "the Chief Musician" of the church.

As an example of the doctrinal precision and clarity he employed, one need only have contact with any of Bach's sacred cantatas. Robert L. Marshall rightly calls Bach's cantatas "musical sermons."[13] These sometimes very short pieces (designed to be played in connection with the preached word in the Sunday service and about 30 minutes long) were designed to adorn the Word of God. They magnificently blend text and melody, always pushing the listener to consider the vertical dimension. Every serious Christian apologist should build a library of Bach's works, especially his cantatas and other sacred works, including the *St. Matthew Passion,* which Terry calls "the deepest, and most moving expression of devotional feeling in the whole of musical literature."[14]

One will also find that gaining a basic literacy in Bach pays dividends not only personally, in enriching the Christian's life of faith in the redeeming Lamb of God, but also broadens the avenues for Gospel preachment to the higher level tender-minded musician, for as Marshall puts it "[h]is most profound appeal is not to the general or even sophisticated *public* but to the *initiated*—by which I mean, quite frankly, to fellow musicians."[15] Bach's music, however, has led such disparate personalities of Goethe, Einstein, Pablo Casals, William F. Buckley, and Albert Schweitzer to pay homage. He is truly, as Karl Geiringer put it, the "culmination of an era"[16] and "a . . . terminal point" (Schweitzer) in that "nothing comes from him; everything merely leads up to him."[17] That this kind of artistic apologetic aids evangelism can be seen in the current phenomenon in otherwise secularized Japan,[18] where an enormous passion for Bach's music has led many to inquire about Christianity, take instruction, and be received into the church.

It can be argued that Bach's place as one of the greatest musicians in history was secured even before he went to his position as church musician in Leipzig in 1723—a position from which he composed most of his cantatas, all of his passions, the colossal *Mass in B Minor,* and a variety of motets and Lutheran masses. This assessment is based on Bach's production before coming to Leipzig, a period during which he composed the *Brandenburg Concerti,* the *Goldberg Variations,* the *Well-Tempered Clavier,* countless organ preludes, sonatas, fugues, toccatas, and suites, as well as numerous concerti for piano, organ, harpsichord, and even the lute, along with solo works for viola, cello, and violin.

Our point is simple: familiarity with Bach brings rewards on many levels to the Christian both personally and as apologist. The astute *fides defensor,* however, will seek to understand the theology that provided the foundation for all of Bach's music and life.[19] To this end, a basic working knowledge of Bach's life is essential. Familiarity with the theological rigor and Christocentric focus of Bach's work is critical so that one can help the tender-minded move from mere wonder at his genius to a grasping of the saving Christ whom Bach sought alone to proclaim. At a time in the Christian church where music has degenerated from its role in the Lutheran Reformation as servant of the Word to technology and Las Vegas-style showmanship, Bach is an anomaly in our day—a self-effacing, theologically literate musician. Only now he is hugely popular.

It is fascinating to note that Bach's enormous standing today is largely attributable to the efforts of Felix Mendelssohn in the nineteenth century. It was Mendelssohn who providentially came into possession of a copy of Bach's *St. Matthew Passion,* a piece that had not been performed since Bach's death in 1750. This passion was performed by Mendelssohn on March 11, 1829, a date from which the rediscovery of Bach can be pinned after a period of almost 80 years where he had been very largely forgotten. Mendelssohn, a convert to Lutheran orthodoxy from Judaism, was solidly in the Reformation camp and even composed an entire symphony dedicated to the celebration of the 300th anniversary of the signing of the Lutheran Augsburg Confession in 1530. In fact, the fourth movement of Mendelssohn's Fifth Symphony in D Major (The "Reformation") is a variation on Luther's *Ein feste Burg ist unser Gott* (A mighty fortress is our God). *Ein feste Burg* was also employed by Bach as the basis for at least two chorales as well as an entire cantata (no. 80).

In Bach and Mendelssohn[20] and their reliance on the theology of Luther and the Lutheran Reformation one finds evidential support for the medieval opinion that theology was "Queen of the Sciences." From a solid theological base came the motivation to create enormous works of musical complexity *(Mass in B Minor)* as well as works of incredible joy and beauty ("Jesu, Joy of Man's Desiring"). Artists in disciplines other than music recognize that in Bach particularly they are in the presence of the sublime and that he points to heaven. The opportunity to move from Bach as composer to Bach as Fifth Evangelist is always present, since Bach viewed himself as a simple servant of the Word. We conclude, appropriately, with the words of another genius, Albert Einstein: "This is what I have to say about Bach's life work: listen, play, love, revere—and keep your mouth shut."[21]

CATHEDRALS AS EVANGELISTS: AN APOLOGETIC MADE IN STONE

Tom Wolfe has captured the state of the arts today and modern man's obsession with reductionism:

> How far we've come! How religiously we've cut away the fat! In the beginning we got rid of nineteenth-century storybook realism. Then we got rid of representational objects. Then we got rid of the third dimension altogether and got really flat

(Abstract Expressionism). Then we got rid of airiness, brush strokes, most of the paint, and the last viruses of drawing and complicated designs (Hard Edge, Color Field, Washington School).

Enough? Hardly, said the Minimalists, who began to come into their own about 1965. Bourgeois connotations, they argued, still hung on to Modern art like a necktie. What about all those nice "lovely" colors that the Hard Edgers and the Color Fielders used? . . .

And how about the painting frame? . . . So Frank Stella turned the canvas itself into a frame and hung it on the wall with nothing in the middle. That got rid of the frames, and the era of "shaped canvases" began.

Sure, but what about this nice sweet bourgeois idea of *hanging up pictures* in the first place . . . all in their nice orderly solid-burgher little rows? . . . So artists like Robert Hunter and Sol Lewitt began painting directly on the gallery walls or on walls outside the gallery window . . .

But what about the wall itself? What about the very idea of a work of art as something "on a wall" at all? How very pre-Modern! . . .

But what about the very idea of the gallery or museum? . . . So began Earth Art, such as Michael Heizer's excavations in the dry lakes of the Mojave Desert and Robert Smithson's *Spiral Jetty* in the Great Salt Lake.

What about the idea of a permanent work of art at all, or even a visible one? Wasn't that the most basic of all assumptions of the Old Order—that art was eternal and composed of objects that could be passed from generation to generation, like Columbus's bones? Out of that objection came Conceptual Art.[22]

Christians, tragically, have fallen headlong into a similar decay in the arts. The reductionism and pietism of modern-day Evangelical Christianity is of course displayed graphically in its music (simplistic, lacking depth, performance-oriented, rarely in a minor key, and, thus, rarely able to speak deeply of sin and death). It is especially displayed in its consumer-driven architecture (strip-mall location and design, minimalistic in the use of the arts, almost sole emphasis architecturally on the horizontal dimension of Christianity [sanctification] to the total exclusion of the vertical [justification]). All is sacrificed at the altar of stewardship of resources and supposedly the preaching of the Gospel, which ends up meaning that as long as Jesus' name is mentioned at the pulpit, the art and architecture of the church is unimportant, for after all, as we say, "we don't worship a building." The presence of a cross becomes unnecessary Roman adornment.

But as culture experiences the corroding effects of 300 years of secularism on the arts, the artistically minded cry out for contact with the sacred. Thus Bach societies proliferate and unbelievers purchase record amounts of crosses and liturgical art. Sales of Gregorian chants are at an all-time high, and pagans stroll by the millions through the great repositories of the artistic tradition of Christendom, lost in amazement at the works of Rembrandt, Dürer, Michelangelo, and Da Vinci. Yet utter reductionism and insipid dullness in the arts still has a home in the architecture of the American Christian church. Make no mistake, the foundations for this condition are not in the *via affirmata* of the Lutheran Reformation but in the twin sources of the *via negativa* of American evangelicalism—pietism and revivalism.

Where are the farsighted churches that see the evangelical value of putting significant financial resources into architecture and art that honors the historic worship of the church? Where are the churches designed and constructed as houses of God and so adorned that those in need of contact with the transcendent come into their sanctuary to sit and gaze in wonder at the beauty and power they are directed to by the architecture? As for those who argue that money would be better used on missions, they should be directed to the great cathedrals of Europe to see the shortsightedness of this argument. Countless are the unbelievers who daily go into these sacred worship spaces and have the stones preach the Gospel to them! For it is in the great cathedrals that the vertical dimension of Christian truth is utterly clear. This objective preaching through veridical architecture is now almost wholly lost in American Christendom.[23]

The arts must again be given their rightful place in the church. We must again demand that our musicians be theologians first. The church must reclaim the position of church musician and should financially support those whose lives are given to the composition of theologically substantive music and works of art employed in the service of Word and Sacrament.

The Christian church militant, in order to go forward to preach the Gospel to all people—including the tender-minded—must first go back and learn from the Lutheran Reformation. There it will find the affirmation of the arts. More important, at the Lutheran Reformation you find the foundation for the arts in a solid incarnational and Christocentric theology. Then perhaps the tender-minded might see, as Tolkien says, that "art has been verified . . . and God is the Lord, of angels, and of men—and of elves. Legend and history have met and fused."[24]

10

LUTHERANS IMITATING EVANGELICALS

Earlier I noted the joy with which we as Evangelicals discovered the Gospel in the Lutheran church. Little did we suspect at the time that Evangelical worship style had already had a deep influence on Lutheran worship style and substance. While our Lutheran church formally assured us of its personal Lutheran orthodoxy and its commitment to the integrity of the liturgy, we began to detect the smell of sulphur on Sunday morning. The same pastor who had presided over the powerful Tenebrae service was "confessional" to us new converts, but unfortunately "church-growth" to other members. Why? Lutherans had been watching Evangelical megachurches grow and glow for decades, and they had been taking notes. Lutherans were envious. Evangelicals must have the answer to growing churches and recapturing vibrancy, Lutherans reasoned. Their worship style must be the key to their success.

An Evangelical worship style, however, cannot properly contain Lutheran substance. It is like serving an excellent and well-aged cabernet sauvignon in a Styrofoam coffee cup. The result of trying to blend Evangelical "style" with Lutheran "substance" inevitably means the loss of Lutheranism. Lutheranism is oriented around the centrality of the Gospel in the ordered service of Word and Sacrament. It focuses on the objectivity of the Gospel and a Christ who comes to us from outside of us primarily to save as we live lives of daily repentance. Evangelical worship does not look to the ancient worship of the church; church history is largely ignored and distrusted. It is subjective in focus, using the Gospel as something the unbeliever needs while using the Law to whip Christians into shape. It fits easily into a market-driven economy based on the felt needs of the chief religious consumer—the most holy and adored Baby Boomer. Instead of taking the good things of Evangelicalism (e.g., its zeal for the lost), Lutheranism for the past two decades or so has been incorporating the crassest and most discredited aspects of Evangelicalism—just as Evangelicals themselves are jettisoning them![1] It shocks Lutherans to learn that Evangelicals generally assume that they are not even saved. Lutherans, however, generally assume Evangelicals are saved, even if perhaps a little off-base theologically. It is not surprising, then, that the influence flows so disproportionately from Evangelicalism to Lutheranism, and not vice versa.

The first inklings of trouble began in the Sunday school at our Lutheran church. We began to receive opposition to the use of the Small Catechism in the grades before confirmation ("What are you trying to do—make them theologians or something?"). The other converts from Evangelicalism to Lutheranism who joined us experienced worse fates. One was removed from his position as a Sunday school teacher for teaching the catechism rather than a curriculum written by Evangelicals and being imposed by the Sunday school superintendent. Two others were ridiculed publicly for taking a stand in support of serious theological education.

THE CHURCH MILITANT
OR MCCHURCH GROWTH?

The dike broke open, however, over the service of Word and Sacrament being transformed into the personal play toy of the congregation's worship committee. Certain church members (generally Baby Boomers who had not been catechized by Luther and Bach but by Focus on the Family and the contemporary Christian music industry) wanted to be seen doing their musical thing up front for all to see. The immediate consequence of this was a de-emphasis on the use of the hymnal in the service ("it's too confusing, and we all know that most people just mouth the words"). It culminated one Sunday when the service omitted Confession and Absolution. At that point one of my daughters turned to me in a moment of clear insight: "We'd better get out of here. We don't even confess our sins anymore." We walked out the center aisle and never looked back.

Her warning was salvific in effect. My wife and I were, however, utterly distraught. Having made the traumatic move from Evangelicalism to Lutheranism a short two years before, we now felt deeply betrayed. Here we were, watching Lutherans doing the very things we had left Evangelicalism to get away from. Lutheran pastors even wrote books with such oxymoronic titles as *Evangelical Style and Lutheran Substance*.[2] We warned our fellow parishioners that the result of this folly would be the loss of a distinctive Lutheran worship form that delivered Lutheran content. In addition, this approach would be repulsive to seeking Evangelicals. Lutheran worship form is to Lutheran substance as fine crystal stemware is to a fine wine. The one is a fit vessel for the other. There is no distinct line where "form" ends and "substance" begins. There is substance in form and form in substance in Lutheran worship.

We learned to our dismay that the Lutheran church was in the midst of a doctrinal war over what some naively thought was only a disagreement about worship style. Some Lutheran pastors are faithful to the liturgy, not seeing it as their personal plaything. Others are Evangelical wanna-bes who tinker with the order of service. Still others are orthodox personally but don't want conflict with their parishioners who are pushing Evangelical worship forms in order to attract numbers. Of course, this is *not* debate about style. It is a war over substance: the confession of Christ and His work.

Our children noted the conflict that our move to Lutheranism had brought. One daughter was midway between seventh and eighth grade when we left this particular Lutheran church. This is not a stable time in a young girl's life even in the best of times. She needed stability at church, and we offered her none. Once again, newfound friends were left at a critical juncture in the lives of our children. Many in the church expressed their complete agreement with our position on the liturgy and catechesis. They truly recognized that the church was on a train that was leaving the station of Lutheranism, and they were in real despair. But they had—or chose to have—little influence. They wanted peace at all costs. To speak up and confront created that hated word among good Lutheran church members—*conflict*. The key positions in the congregation were controlled by those who were Lutheran in formal affiliation but thoroughly Evangelical in all that mattered.

To say that these people were Evangelical, however, is far too much of a compliment. The Evangelical worship style of these Lutherans was so tacky—so "seventies"—that we became too embarrassed to invite serious Evangelicals to our church. Real Evangelicals could see through this nonsense. We started to invite Evangelicals only if we knew in advance that the service was to be from the hymnal.

The Lutheran church is at war, and the result is a wild inconsistency in her churches.[3] There are Lutheran churches trying to do a service largely indistinguishable from Evangelical megachurches like Willow Creek. Then one can find wonderfully orthodox

Lutheran churches led by faithful pastors. I have the greatest respect for solid confessional Lutheran pastors and laymen. They introduced me to orthodox Lutheranism and catechized me into Lutheranism's theology of the cross. Men like John Warwick Montgomery, Rod Rosenbladt, David Schleusener, Charles Cortwright, Arthur Just, Randy Golter, Bill Cwirla, Harold Senkbeil, and the staff of *Logia* magazine[4] continue as true beacons for Reformation Lutheranism. My library shows the marks of that solid Lutheran theology. Works by older theologians like C. F. W. Walther, Francis Pieper, and J. T. Mueller, and more recently Gene Edward Veith and David Scaer have been invaluable.[5] Tragically, however, the five Lutheran churches we tried in our area gave us no final reason to have left Evangelicalism in the first place.

Our local Lutheran church was going in a direction my wife and I found repulsive. We wanted Lutheran orthodoxy centered around Scripture, faithfully reflected in an orthodox hymnal, liturgy, and catechism. More centrally, because we wanted a church of the Gospel, we wanted a church that honored historical worship and instruction that flowed in and out of the doctrine of justification. Many felt the same. We discussed with others starting a mission church. Ultimately God directed our steps in other ways.

FINDING ORTHODOXY

An Evangelical convert to Lutheranism can spot an Evangelical fox in the Lutheran hen house with no difficulty. Signs include the role the hymnal plays in the service, the place of the sacraments in the life of the church, and the emphasis on a serious pursuit of the Word of God through mastery of the Small Catechism. The place that the three books of Lutheranism—Bible, hymnal, and catechism—play in the life of a church can tell you all you need to know about that church's commitment to, and future in, Lutheranism.

We had noticed a small Lutheran church in town. A friend of ours decided to visit this church on a spy mission. His analysis was swift. This church was carrying forward the Lutheran Reformation. Several others visited and confirmed that the pastor did the liturgy well, with passion and attention to aesthetics. The liturgy was not a plaything. The sermon was Christocentric and distinguished Law and Gospel clearly. Confirmation was a full examination in public of the catechumens. In short, the congregation was a refreshing throwback to how I suspect many Lutheran churches had been only 20 years ago. Reluctantly, we moved again.

One daughter was in the middle of catechism. She did not like this move at all. However, *via sola gratia* we found in the pastor an unflinching commitment to orthodox Lutheranism and not a lip-service Lutheranism rolled out only for enthused converts.

We simply wanted what we had assumed all Lutherans stood for—Christ-centered worship by means of the historic liturgy and serious catechesis and study of the Word for believers. We were not looking for more vibrant youth groups, snazzier church schools, tastier potlucks, or warmer fellowship groups. We were looking for evangelism that stressed conversion and not recruitment through sales methods. Certain Lutheran churches do give the seeking Evangelical an uncluttered look at confessional Lutheranism. Even though I am a lawyer, you can trust me on this one: seeking Evangelicals *will* find these churches.[6]

When dealing with man's sinful nature and his desire to do what "sells" in order to generate numbers, *caveat emptor* always applies. That is, beware of the Evangelical addiction to church-growth marketing techniques. Some Lutheran churches are also infected with this disease. The presence of the hymnal and catechesis are only pointers—they help ensure that the structure of Lutheranism is in place. Or as Hermann Sasse puts it, Lutheranism is the lamp stand on which the lamp of the Gospel is placed:

> It so happens that the people who lived in the Age of the Reformation knew and understood certain truths which were later forgotten and had to be learned from them again. The loyalty of the Evangelical Lutheran Church is accounted for by

these experiences. We are faithful to this church, not because it is the church of our Fathers, but because it is the church of the Gospel; not because it is the church of Luther, but because it is the church of Jesus Christ. If it became something else, if its teaching were something else than a correct exposition of the plain Word of God, it would no longer be our church. It is not the Lutheran liturgy that matters. The church can get along without it if it must. It is not the Symbolic Books that count. If it should ever be demonstrated that their exposition of the Gospel is false, that they contain essential errors, we would be the first ones to cast them into the fire, for our *norma normans,* the standard by which we judge doctrines, is the Bible alone. Nor is it the Evangelical Lutheran Church, as a separate church in Christendom, that matters. The moment it becomes anything else than the stand on which is put the lamp which alone is a light upon our path, it becomes a sect and must disappear. We would not be Lutherans if we did not believe this![7]

CONCLUSION
WHICH WAY FOR LUTHERANISM?

In these pages I have traced my own spiritual pilgrimage from Evangelicalism to the evangel—the Gospel of Jesus Christ as proclaimed and presented in its purest form in the Lutheran church. I have also described a Christ-centered basis for apologetics, one that does not depend upon faulty and unscriptural presuppositions about the place of human reason in conversion. Finally, I have sounded a warning! It remains for me now to say a brief word about the state of the Lutheran church and its place in American Christianity. Consider these words:

> Lutherans do have much to offer to the wider American community, but only if they can fulfill two conditions. First, to contribute as Lutherans in America, Lutherans must remain authentically Lutherans. Second, to contribute as Lutherans in America, Lutherans must also find out how to speak Lutheranism with an American accent. Falling short of either condition means that, though Lutherans as religious individuals may contribute much to Christianity in America, there will be no distinctively *Lutheran* contribution. The task is to steer between the Scylla of assimilation without tradition and the Charybdis of tradition without assimilation. If such skillful navigation could take place, the resources that Lutherans offer

to Americans, especially to other Protestants, would be of incalculable benefit.[1]

Remarkably, this statement comes not from the pen of a Lutheran but from the pen of Mark Noll, professor of history at Wheaton College, a citadel of American Evangelicalism. Yet Noll perfectly summarizes Lutheranism's historic opportunity. Lutherans must turn up the Lutheran thermostat, learn to speak with "an American accent" (i.e., move out of ethnic isolationism), and stop their flirtation with the worst church-growth techniques. If it does not, American Lutheranism as we know it will justifiably perish. And if it does, Noll warns, all American churches will suffer. At present, many Lutherans are hell-bent on eating the rancid and discarded leftovers of Evangelical church-growth programs. At the same time, however, God is bringing about a real revival of confessional Lutheran orthodoxy. This provides the only hope of both restoring the evangel to higher-level Evangelicals, while simultaneously rescuing it from lower-level Evangelicals. Theologically and liturgically lukewarm Lutheranism offers nothing to Evangelicals. They will spew it out of their mouths. And rightly so. But an authentic church with the blood of Luther in its veins, a church where the Gospel is preached in all its truth and purity, a church where the sacraments are rightly administered, a church where the historic liturgy is celebrated with gravity and joy, a church where theologically profound hymns are sung, a church where the young are taught real doctrine, a church where the old are respected and cared for—that church will not only provide a spiritual home for the wandering Evangelicals but will also raise up a flag to which all embattled Christians may rally.

I have attempted to sound a clarion call to the Lutheran church to be Lutheran. It provides the soundest hope for the Evangelical believer. It certainly did for me as a confused Evangelical. I have also attempted to sound a call to the reclaiming of a distinctively Lutheran apologetic for both the tough- and tender-minded unbeliever. For the tough-minded I have advocated an objective, evidential, juridical, and Christocentric defense of the faith that arises from the Lutheran Reformation and its emphasis on the centrality of the incarnation and the cross. For the tender-minded I have pointed to the work of the literary apologists and the music of Bach and Mendelssohn, all of which support Tolkien's assertion that the Gospel "has the supremely convincing tone of Primary Art, that is, of Creation."[2]

Lutheranism has a unique message and unique books for both the tough- and tender-minded. For the tough-minded it offers Luther's Small Catechism. For the tender-minded it offers its fine arts and the historic liturgy—a place where heaven and earth meet.

As Christians we truly "stand on the shoulders of giants." We have the benefit of learning from the greatest intellects who have addressed issues of truth and defended the faith with great ability and clarity through the centuries. Much remains to be done in our own day. Luther was surely correct in saying that if we do not preach the Gospel to the needs of our own day, then we don't preach the Gospel at all. A strong warning. Yet we find that God in His mercy gives us grace to faithfully preach this saving Gospel to our own day. Thus we, too, will end our life's toil and enter the church triumphant as Bach ended his compositions, with the letters S.D.G.—*Soli Deo Gloria* (To God alone be the glory). While we remain in the church militant, we live by the two letters Bach used many times at the beginning of his pieces: J.J.—*Jesu Juva* (Jesus help me). Amen.

Appendix A

A NARRATIVE COMMENTARY ON THE DIVINE SERVICE*

JOHN T. PLESS

INTRODUCTION

The high and holy worship of God is faith in Jesus Christ. Such faith is created and sustained by God's Service to us. In the Divine Service, the Lord comes to us in His Word and Sacrament to bless and enliven us with His gifts. The Service is not something we do for God, but His service to us received in faith. The liturgy is God's work. He gives, we receive (John 4:20–26; Hebrews 8:1–6).

INVOCATION

From God's Word we know that wherever God puts His name, there He is to bless. In the Old Testament the temple was the place where God graciously caused His name to be present (1 Kings 8:27–30).

God has put His name—Father, Son, and Holy Spirit on us in Holy Baptism. The Divine Service begins "In the name of the Father and of the Son and of the Holy Spirit." Every Divine Service is for the hallowing of the Lord's name, which the Small Catechism reminds us is done "when the Word of God is taught in its truth and purity, and we, as the children of God, also lead holy lives according to it" (Matthew 28:18–20).

CONFESSION AND ABSOLUTION

It is only through the forgiveness of sins that we enter into the life of heaven. To confess our sins is to speak the truth about our lives. God seeks that truth in the heart and on the lips. To confess our sin is to say "Amen" to God's just verdict that we have sinned against Him and so deserve only death and hell (1 John 1:8–10).

The truth of our sinfulness is answered by the truth of God's forgiveness for the sake of the suffering and death of His Son. From the lips of a man "called and ordained" as a servant of the Word, we hear God Himself speaking absolution, that is, the forgiveness of sins. To that forgiveness faith says, "Amen," that is, "Truth." *Amen* is the great word of worship; it indicates that the gift has been received (John 20:19–23).

INTROIT

Having received the Lord's forgiveness, we are glad to enter into His courts with praise and thanksgiving. This entrance is made in the Introit with the Lord's own words, most often drawn from the Psalms (Psalm 100).

KYRIE, HYMN OF PRAISE

Kyrie eleison is a Greek phrase meaning "Lord, have mercy." In the Kyrie we come before the King of mercy with the prayer that was on the lips of Blind Bartimaeus, whom Jesus healed. We approach our merciful Savior and King as citizens of heaven, seeking His mercy for our salvation, the peace of the whole world, the well-being of His church, our worship, and our everlasting defense (Mark 10:49).

The Lord to whom we cry for mercy is the Savior who has come to us in the flesh. "Glory to God in the highest, and peace to His people on earth" echoes the hymn that the high angels of God sang to the shepherds at Bethlehem. In this hymn we acclaim and extol the Son of God who humbled Himself to be our brother and now reigns over us as Savior from the right hand of His Father. An alternate to this hymn is "This Is the Feast of Victory," taken from the Book of Revelation. This hymn proclaims the victory of the Lamb who was crucified for us. (Luke 2:14; Revelation 5:11–14).

SALUTATION, COLLECT OF THE DAY

The pastor stands in the congregation as Christ's servant. The vestments he wears indicate that he is not speaking on his own but as one sent and authorized to represent Christ Jesus. As the authorized representative of the Lord he says, "The Lord be with you." The congregation responds, "And also with you." Pastor and congregation are bound together in this salutation, or greeting, as the pastor prays the Collect of the Day on behalf of the gathered congregation (2 Timothy 4:22).

The Collect is a short prayer that "collects" in one short petition all it is that we are asking God to do for us on the basis of the Word that we are about to hear—read and preached (Philippians 4:6).

OLD TESTAMENT READING, GRADUAL, EPISTLE, VERSE, HOLY GOSPEL, HYMN OF THE DAY, SERMON

In Ephesians 4, the apostle Paul tells us that the ascended Christ gave gifts to His church: apostles, prophets, evangelists, and pastor-teachers. These gifts are made manifest in the Divine Service as we hear God's Word read and proclaimed. First, we hear from a prophet in the words of the Old Testament Reading. After the deacon reads the Scripture, he proclaims: "This is the Word of the Lord." The Lord's Word is embraced by the congregation's response of thanksgiving: "Thanks be to God." In this way, the church confesses Holy Scripture for what it is—the Word of God. The Gradual, selected verses of Scripture, is sung by the congregation. The Gradual is a "bridge of praise" that links the Old Testament with the New Testament. Second, we hear from an apostle in the words of a New Testament Epistle. From the apostle we are given the truth that is in Jesus for our faith and life. The "Alleluia Verse" is taken from John 6:68. This Verse is our anticipation of the Lord who comes to us in His words, words that are spirit and life. Third, we hear from an evangelist in the words of the Holy Gospel. In the words of the evangelist we are given the Word of Life, Jesus Christ. The congregation acknowledges the Lord's presence in His Gospel by standing and extolling His glory and praising Him. The praise continues in the Hymn of the Day. As the Word of God dwells in us, it calls forth songs of faith and love. This hymn reflects the particular theme of the Scripture Readings that we have heard. Fourth, in continuity with the prophets, apostles, and evangelists, our pastor stands in our midst to deliver the Lord's Law and Gospel in the sermon. He is God's mouth for the congregation as through him the Good Shepherd's voice sounds forth to call, gather, and enlighten His flock (Ephesians 4:11; Colossians 3:16; John 6:63; Luke 10:16).

NICENE CREED

Having heard the Word of God, we confess our faith in His name. The Creed is our saying back to God what He has first said to us. In the Nicene Creed we acclaim the truth of the triune God and His work of salvation accomplished for us in His incarnate Son, Jesus Christ (Matthew 10:32–33; Philippians 2:11).

THE PRAYER OF THE CHURCH

God's Word is always primary in worship. We speak only as we are spoken to. Gathered in Jesus' name, we bring the petitions and thanksgivings before Him that grow out of His Word. This prayer is called the Prayer of the Church for in it the royal priesthood of all believers does its priestly work of making "requests, prayers, intercession and thanksgiving" for all people, "for kings and all those in authority, that we may live peaceful and quiet lives in all godliness and holiness" (1 Timothy 2:1–6).

OFFERING, OFFERTORY

Having received from the generosity of the Father who is the author and giver of every good and perfect gift, we now give of the gifts that we have been given. The Offering is accompanied with an Offertory from Psalm 116 that teaches us that the highest offering is simply to receive, in faith, the cup of salvation from the Lord's hand (Psalm 116:12–14, 17–19).

PREFACE, SANCTUS, PRAYER, OUR FATHER

Drawn toward the gifts of Jesus' body and blood, our hearts are lifted up in thanksgiving and praise as we anticipate the reception of the gifts that carry with them our redemption. The Sanctus brings together the song of heaven's angels in adoration of the holy Three in One and the acclamations of Palm Sunday: "Blessed is He who comes in the name of the Lord! Hosanna in the highest!" In the prayer we give thanks to the Lord for the redemption that He has secured for us by His cross; we ask Him to prepare us to receive that redemption in living and joyful faith. The Our Father, the prayer that Jesus taught His disciples to pray, is the "table prayer" with which we come to the Lord's Table (Lamentations 3:41; Luke 21:28; Isaiah 6:3; Mark 11:9–10).

CONSECRATION, PAX DOMINI, AGNUS DEI, DISTRIBUTION

The pastor speaks the Lord's own words; these words give and bestow what they declare, the body and blood of Christ. The Sacrament of Jesus' body and blood is the vehicle for peace. Showing them His wounds, the risen Lord declared His peace to His disciples on Easter evening. That same peace is given to us with the Lord's body and blood. By sharing the "peace of the Lord" with each other, we lay aside all that stands in contradiction with the Lord's testament. With the words of John the Baptist, the Agnus Dei confesses the mercy and peace that we receive from the Lamb of God in His Supper. We come to the Lord's Table hungry and thirsty, and He feeds us with His body and refreshes us with His blood. It is the Lord's Supper. As Luther reminds us, "Our Lord is at one and the same time chef, cook, butler, host, and food" (1 Corinthians 11:23–26; John 20:21; John 1:29).

POST-COMMUNION CANTICLE, PRAYER

Having received the Lord's body and blood for our salvation, like Simeon who held in his arms the Savior of the world, we go in peace and joy, singing Simeon's song from Luke 2. Another song of thanksgiving, based on 1 Chronicles 16:8–10, may be used instead. Before we leave the Lord's Table, we give thanks, asking that the salutary gift of Jesus' body and blood would have its way in our lives, strengthening us in faith toward God and fervent love toward one another. The Sacrament draws us outside of ourselves to live in Christ by faith and in the neighbor by love, to paraphrase Luther (Luke 2:29–32).

BENEDICTION, HYMN

The name of the Lord is the beginning and the end of the Divine Service. We are now marked with the Lord's name in the Benediction—that word of God's blessing from Numbers 6 in which He favors us with His grace and peace. With the Lord's name given us in Holy Baptism, we were drawn together. Now, with that same name, He sends us back into the world, to the places of our various callings, to live by the mercy we have received as living sacrifices to the praise of His glory and the good of our neighbor (Numbers 6:22–27; Romans 12:1–2).

*Based on the liturgy as printed in *Lutheran Worship,* the hymnal of The Lutheran Church—Missouri Synod.

Appendix B

FOR FURTHER STUDY

ANNOTATED BIBLIOGRAPHY OF APOLOGETICAL AND THEOLOGICAL LITERATURE

Anderson, J. N. D. *Christianity and Comparative Religion.* Downers Grove: IVP, 1977. One of the great authorities on world religions explains what makes Christianity fundamentally different from other world religions.

Archer, Gleason. *Encyclopedia of Bible Difficulties.* Grand Rapids: Eerdmans, 1982. A must-buy volume. Archer was professor of Old Testament at Trinity Seminary and exceptionally well qualified in Semitic languages to do a work of this scope.

Bolt, Robert. *A Man for All Seasons.* New York: Vintage Books, 1960. A marvelous book and a must-see film and play about the life of Sir Thomas More. Though an ardent Catholic who considered Luther an enemy, More was on the side of the angels during the reign of the supposedly "Protestant" Henry VIII.

Bruce, F. F. *The New Testament Documents: Are They Reliable?* Grand Rapids: Eerdmans, 1987. Perhaps the best short treatment of the subject.

Butler, Samuel. *The Way of All Flesh.* New York: The Modern Library, Random House, 1950. This work is a kind of hilarious travelogue of one who saw through the false piety of "professional" religious people. It is considered to be Butler's autobiography of his journey out of English "evangelical" Christianity into full-blown secularism.

Camus, Albert. *The Plague.* New York: Alfred A. Knopf, 1948. Considered to be perhaps the most important novel to come out of postwar Europe. Camus brilliantly describes the choices available to those who have rejected a Christian conception of the universe. For those wondering about the power of the objective Gospel to save, see the book by the pastor of the American Church in Paris who presents the evidence that Camus earnestly desired Christian Baptism just before Camus's tragic death in an auto accident in 1960 (Howard Mumma, *Albert Camus and the Minister* [Brewster, Mass.: Paraclete Press, 2000]). Mumma, sadly, displays a thoroughly unscholarly doctrine of the accuracy of Scripture which, thankfully, Camus appeared to have successfully ignored.

Carnell, Edward John. *An Introduction to Christian Apologetics.* Grand Rapids: Eerdmans, 1948. Carnell was one of the founding fathers of Fuller Seminary during its glory days. Brilliant and yet very disturbed psychologically toward the end of his life, Carnell is always worth reading. This work is one of the really fine overviews of apologetics.

Chesterton, G. K. *The Everlasting Man*. New York: Dodd, Mead & Co., 1925. A Catholic apologist of more than average interest. His renowned "Father Brown" detective stories make wonderful gifts for unbelievers who can later be more easily persuaded to look into Chesterton's theological writings, such as *Orthodoxy* (New York: Garden City Publishing, 1908).

Crews, Frederick C. *The Pooh Perplex*. New York: E. P. Dutton & Co., 1963. The Pooh story is brilliantly examined in a hilarious manner by various "sophisticated" schools of literary interpretation (e.g., Marxist, Freudian, etc.) in order to find its "true" meaning. For example, Crews—a professor of English at UCLA at the time and writing under an ecclesiastical pseudonym—pens one chapter entitled "The Sacramental Meaning of Winnie-the-Pooh." This book is a postmodernist's nightmare.

Flew, Anthony. *God and Philosophy: An Audit of the Case for Christian Theism*. New York: Harcourt, Brace & World, Inc., 1966. Flew is a renowned atheist who has debated Gary Habermas and others on the claims of Christianity. As an analytical philosopher in the vein of A. J. Ayer, Flew claims that there is insufficient evidence for Christian belief and no basis on which to ground its claims. The major thrust of the book is captured in his "Parable of the Two Explorers."

Geisler, Norman. *The Roots of Evil*. Grand Rapids: Zondervan, 1978. Deals with the various approaches to the problem and shows how biblical theism provides the most comprehensive solution. See also C. S. Lewis on this subject in a book entitled *The Problem of Pain* (New York: MacMillan Publishers, 1962).

Geisler, Norman, and William Nix. *A General Introduction to the Bible*. Chicago: Moody Press, 1968. Covers the issues of inspiration, canonicity, text, and translation of the Bible. Excellent general reference work.

Grisham, John. *The Testament*. New York: Doubleday, 1999. The famous novelist shows his ability to produce a literary work of solid apologetical value. Not often do you find a Christian (let alone a missionary) portrayed so positively in literature. That the Christian is used in this novel in a redemptive fashion in the life of a jaded and usually well-lubricated trial lawyer/protagonist is even more fascinating. An excellent protoevangelion for unbelieving friends.

Hanson, Victor, and John Heath. *Who Killed Homer? The Demise of Classical Education and the Recovery of Greek Wisdom*. New York: Free Press, 1998. An excellent secular analysis of how classical studies have been destroyed in the university and the surprising conclusion as to the identity of the true culprit. This is a "must read" done by two insiders at the highest levels of current academia. Typical of the marvelous prose style is the following description of bureaucrats in academia who hide their mediocrity behind tenure and would not know classical education if it had a sign on it: "We would require administrators themselves to teach a class or two a year and stay put for ten. Today they have become an entirely new itinerant class, whose offices, dress, attitude, and speech instantly give them away as a bureaucratic overclass who do not read, write, or teach. Likewise, the 'walking resume,' who has been at five universities in six years and taught intensively at none, would suffer the disgrace he has earned." May true teachers such as Hanson and Heath increase!

Hawthorne, Nathaniel. *The Scarlet Letter.* New York: Houghton Mifflin Co., 1963. A tremendous illustration of the fact that Puritan New England was not the "kingdom of God on earth" that contemporary pro-American Christians make it out to be.

Hertzberg, Arthur. *The French Enlightenment and the Jews.* New York: Columbia University Press, 1968. A former professor of history at Columbia and a Rabbi, Hertzberg shows how the roots of modern anti-Semitism were fully formed in the secular French Enlightenment. Decimates the modern mantra that Christianity, and more particularly the Reformation, gave birth to racial hatred of the Jews.

Hick, John. *The Existence of God.* New York: MacMillan, 1960. Contains the historic debate on the existence of God done on BBC between Bertrand Russell and Father Frederick Coppleston. This work has several polemical anti-Christian essays.

Hoover, A. J. *Don't You Believe It!* Chicago: Moody Press, 1972. How to pinpoint faulty reasoning. Special reference is made to the logical pitfalls that many Christians fall prey to in dialogue with intelligent unbelief.

James, William. *The Varieties of Religious Experience.* London: Longmans, Green, 1907. James, professor of psychology at Harvard at the turn of this century, explains religious conversion in purely psychological terms. For an excellent critique of this work, see John Warwick Montgomery's essay on James in *The Shape of the Past.* Minneapolis: Bethany Books, 1975.

Johnson, Phillip. *Darwin on Trial.* Downers Grove: IVP, 1991. This professor of evidence at Boalt Hall Law School at UC Berkeley puts Darwin on the witness stand and finds his theory to be seriously lacking in admissible evidence. The best popular critique of Darwinism.

Kittleson, James. *Luther the Reformer: The Story of the Man and His Career.* Minneapolis: Augsburg, 1986. The best and most complete biography of Luther since Roland Bainton's *Here I Stand!: A Life of Martin Luther* (New York: Abingdon-Cokesbury Press, 1950). Obtain at all costs. Kittleson was a student of Lewis Spitz at Stanford (Spitz is the author of the superb two-volume work on the era entitled *The Renaissance and Reformation Movements* [Chicago: Rand McNally & Co., 1972] and a former professor of history at Ohio State University).

Koestler, Arthur. *The Lotus and the Robot.* New York: Harper Books, 1960. Documents Koestler's pilgrimage to the founts of Eastern wisdom. Unfortunately Koestler found nothing but utter selfishness and greed. Koestler is a particularly pathetic example of what can happen when one attempts to "experience" the maximum number of religious and philosophical positions in a lifetime. Koestler and his wife committed simultaneous suicide. See also Koestler's *Darkness at Noon* (New York: Random House, 1941) for a chilling account of his disillusionment with Marxism and other efforts at political salvation.

Lewis, C. S. *Christian Reflections.* Grand Rapids: Eerdmans, 1967. Worth the price of the book just for the chapter entitled "Modern Theology and Biblical Criticism." Other chapters on "The Poison of Subjectivism" and "On Church Music" make this must reading.

————. *God in the Dock.* Grand Rapids: Eerdmans, 1970. A fascinating collection of essays on everything from apologetics and animal suffering to capital punishment and the value of reading old books.

————. *A Grief Observed.* New York: Seabury Press, 1961. Lewis writes with haunting reality concerning the events surrounding his wife's death from cancer. An excellent book for unbelievers who are coping with personal tragedy.

————. *Mere Christianity.* New York: MacMillan & Co., 1970. Twenty-fifth printing at that time! Now widely considered to be the single most influential popular defense of historic Christianity done in the twentieth century. Its impact on bringing down the walls of unbelief is simply incalculable.

————. *Surprised By Joy.* London: Geoffrey Bles, 1955. A rare commodity—a nonrepulsive conversion story. Lewis says he was brought "kicking and struggling" into the Christian faith based on the sheer weight of the evidence alone. Not your garden variety insipid Christian testimonial. This makes an excellent gift for the "higher level tender-minded" unbeliever for whom the world of art, literature, poetry, and music point to the sacred.

Lindsell, Harold. *The Battle for the Bible.* Grand Rapids: Zondervan, 1976. This work (and its sequel, *The Bible in the Balance,* also published by Zondervan, in 1979) created a major ruckus in Evangelical circles upon its release. As a founding member of Fuller Seminary and former editor-in-chief of *Christianity Today* magazine, Lindsell was in an advantageous position to comment on the view of Holy Writ taken at various seminaries and Bible colleges in the United States. Lindsell knew where all the bones were buried in the inerrancy debate within Evangelicalism in the 1970s and had devastating factual information on Evangelical organizations like Young Life and Fuller Seminary (which is a major seminary feed for Young Life), whose stance on the total reliability of Scripture is either weasel-like or one of concerted disinterest.

Linnemann, Eta. *Historical Criticism of the Bible: Methodology or Ideology?* Grand Rapids: Baker Books, 1990. The remarkable story of a prominent historical-critical theologian who was a prized pupil of Bultmann and Fuchs in Germany but who came to see the error of her ways and the utterly unscholarly approach to the biblical material taken by her teachers. Linnemann followed Bultmann to the logical conclusion—the loss of the Gospel itself and then to the loss of all hope in this world in the here and now. Though inducted into the prestigious Society for New Testament Studies, she became an alcoholic and lived in total despair until she heard the Gospel, repented, believed, and was saved. The book is worthwhile for the introduction alone where Linnemann pleads with the reader to do her a favor and throw away her earlier best-selling books and articles as utter poison!

Luther, Martin. Small Catechism. A theological classic that deserves to be studied and treasured by every Christian. Learn this short catechism, and you will know more Christian doctrine than many Evangelical pastors. Note to concerned Christian parents: If you have yet to find a clear and thoroughly Christocentric presentation of the faith that can be memorized by an 8-year-old child or an 80-year-old grandparent, look no further. Both the Wisconsin Evangelical Lutheran Synod (WELS) and the Lutheran Church—Missouri Synod (LCMS) have excellent versions. WELS materials are available through Northwestern Publishing House in Milwaukee, Wisconsin, while the LCMS publication arm is Concordia Publishing House in St. Louis, Missouri. Personally, my favorite edition is the 1983 version produced by the Minnesota District of WELS and available only through the Martin Luther College bookstore in New Ulm, Minnesota. It simply presents Luther's words without all the later accretions provided by well-meaning, but generally less lucid and always more verbose, commentators. It is also illustrated and quite compact, thus preserving the integrity of the critical modifier *small!*

Machen, J. Gresham. *Christianity and Liberalism.* Grand Rapids: Eerdmans, 1956. This work is probably the single most devastating critique of liberal Christianity ever done.

Martin, Michael. *The Case against Christianity.* Philadelphia: Temple University Press, 1991. Perhaps the most important effort since Bertrand Russell's *Why I Am Not a Christian* (New York: Simon & Schuster, 1957). Martin, a professor of philosophy at Boston University, attempts to attack both the philosophical and evidential arguments for Christian faith.

Mayer, F. E. *The Religious Bodies of America.* St. Louis: Concordia Publishing House, 1961—but still in print! Excellent summary of the basic doctrinal teachings of the three branches of the Christian church. If you want a concise description of the differences, for example, between Calvinists and Lutherans on the Lord's Supper, Baptism, or election, this is a must-buy for you. A wide variety of sects and isms are also competently handled.

Modern Reformation. Alliance of Confessing Evangelicals, 1716 Spruce Street, Philadelphia, 19103. www.AllianceNet.org. A theological journal committed to bringing the insights of the sixteenth-century Reformation to the twentieth-century church. Michael Horton, editor, studied at Biola and knows American Evangelicalism. This journal is Reformed (Calvinist) in basic orientation, though Lutherans and others do contribute articles and Horton himself is better on Luther than most Lutherans writing on the reformer! For a journal committed to the insights of the Lutheran Reformation, see *Logia,*

A Journal of Lutheran Theology (15825, 373rd Avenue, Northville, South Dakota, 57465. www.logia.org).

Montgomery, John Warwick. *Christianity for the Tough-Minded.* Minneapolis: Bethany Books, 1973. Essays in support of an intellectually defensible religious commitment. Montgomery is the foremost apologist of our day. He holds 10 earned degrees and is both an American attorney and an English barrister as well as an ordained Lutheran clergyman (LCMS) and author of more than 50 books on the defense of the Christian faith.

————. *History and Christianity.* Minneapolis: Bethany Books, 1964. This book was reprinted by the Canadian Institute for Law, Theology, and Public Policy in 2002 under the title of *History, Law, and Christianity.* It is Montgomery's best-known work. It contains an excellent section on the reliability of the New Testament documents as well as the transcript of one of Montgomery's numerous (and infamous) debates with unfortunate opponents. C. S. Lewis read this work and wrote that "it couldn't be bettered."

————. *The Law above the Law.* Minneapolis: Bethany Books, 1975. This volume explains why the law needs biblical foundations and why Christians need the evidentiary perspective of the law. The appendix contains a rare reprint of Professor Simon Greenleaf's classic work, *The Testimony of the Evangelists.* Greenleaf was professor of evidence at the Harvard Law School in the nineteenth-century and the greatest living authority at that time on common law evidence. Greenleaf puts the Gospel writers in the witness box and finds them to be utterly unimpeachable.

————. *Myth, Allegory and Gospel.* Minneapolis: Bethany Books, 1974. Essays by four scholars interpreting the works of C. S. Lewis, J. R. R. Tolkien, G. K. Chesterton, and Charles Williams. Must reading for those interested in evangelizing the higher level tender-minded unbeliever.

————. *The Shaping of America.* Minneapolis: Bethany Books, 1981. Fascinating critique of the elements that have gone into the shaping of American Christianity.

————. *The Suicide of Christian Theology.* Minneapolis: Bethany Books, 1975. Included in this volume is the transcript of Montgomery's epic debate with death-of-God theologian Thomas J. J. Altizer. The "Death of God" school led by Altizer never recovered from that night at Rockefeller Chapel on the campus of the University of Chicago. You won't regret the purchase.

————. *Tractatus Logico-Theologicus.* Bonn, Germany: Science and Culture Publications, 2002. Montgomery's magnum opus in apologetics. The apologetical equivalent of Bach's *Mass in B Minor.* Don't be put off by the name—it plays off a similar title by the greatest philosopher of the twentieth century, Ludwig Wittgenstein. While Wittgenstein properly concluded that human effort could not produce a transcendent philosophy or ethic, Montgomery shows how the unbeliever simply must deal with the truth claims of Christianity and that an unbiased weighing of those evidences takes the honest inquirer to the foot of the cross and then to transcendence. Truly the *Mere Christianity* for twenty-first-century man.

————. *The Transcendent Holmes.* Ashcroft, British Columbia: Calabash Press, 2000. Besides examining long-debated problems within Holmesian circles (i.e., the true location of 221B Baker Street, how many times was Watson married, where was Watson wounded, what we know of Holmes's brother Mycroft, etc.), these articles examine the fascinating issues surrounding Holmes's evolving religious position. Montgomery develops the evidence for the position that Holmes's journey to Tibet after the incident with Moriarty at Reichenbach most assuredly did *not* result in Holmes either remaining in rationalism or moving toward Eastern mysticism. In fact, in a startling conclusion, a dialogue between Watson and Holmes on ultimate religious questions shows why Holmes's appeal, like that of Bach, continues to cut across cultures—because it is archetypal and thus fully "transcendent."

Outler, Albert. *John Wesley.* New York: Oxford University Press, 1964. The definitive biography on Wesley. Excellent materials on Wesley's unfortunate—and unbiblical—doctrine of Christian perfection and the disastrous results when sanctification is allowed to swallow up justification. Wesley's book on sanctification says it all in the title—*A Plain Account of Christian Perfection* (London: Epworth Press, 1952). It is in the latter work that "sins" become "mistakes."

Parton, Craig. *Richard Whately: A Man for All Seasons.* Edmonton, Alberta, Canada: Canadian Institute for Law, Theology, and Public Policy, 1997. Whately was an able defender of the faith during the time of David Hume. With great genius and sarcasm, Whately applies Hume's own flawed methodology to the life of Napoléon and concludes that Napoléon never existed! Napoléon just happened to be alive and in exile at the time on the Island of Elba. This work, therefore, contains an actual reprint of Whately's apologetical classic entitled "Historic Doubts Relative to Napoleon Buonaparte." The critical apologetical point is made that presuppositional bias (in Hume's case it was bias against even the possibility of miracles occurring) must never be allowed to frustrate factual inquiry.

Sasse, Hermann. *This Is My Body.* Adelaide, South Australia: Open Book, 1977. Worth buying just to read a lucid and great scholar present the biblical, historical, and theological basis for Luther's contention concerning the real presence of Christ in the Lord's Supper. This is the only book that recreates a "transcript" of the historic debate in Marburg on October 1–4, 1529 between Luther and Zwingli concerning the meaning of the words "This is My body." An excellent illustration of the legal principle of always going with facts over "logic" if a conflict between the two appears to arise. Shows Luther's unwaivering stand on the clarity, importance, and authority of every word of Scripture.

Sayers, Dorothy. *The Whimsical Christian.* New York: MacMillan Publishing, 1978. Dorothy Sayers is known to many as a superb mystery writer, translator of Dante, and playwright. Few know her as one of the truly fine Christian apologists of the twentieth century. This collection of 18 essays covers topics ranging from Sherlock Holmes to Faust to Christian liturgy. She should inspire a generation of female defenders of the faith.

Schaff, Philip. *The Creeds of Christendom.* 3 vols. Grand Rapids: Baker Books, 1983. A history and commentary on the historic creeds of the three main branches of the Christian church (Catholic, Orthodox, and Protestant).

Senkbeil, Harold. *Sanctification: Christ in Action.* Milwaukee: Northwestern Publishing House, 1992. This fascinating little book presents how the Reformation views the doctrine of sanctification and how that looks when put side by side with the predominate Evangelical view as seen in the writings of Charles Swindoll. This book may get you rethinking what you hear taught about the Christian life on radio and TV, let alone from some of America's most popular authors and speakers.

Sherwin-White, A. N. *Roman Society and Roman Law in the New Testament.* Oxford: Clarendon Press, 1963. A reprint of a series of lectures given in 1960–61 by a scholar in Roman law and culture at Oxford. The author examines the New Testament in light of his vast knowledge of Roman civilization and finds that the Gospel writings ring with the stamp of authenticity.

Sire, James. *The Universe Next Door.* Downers Grove: IVP, 1979. A catalogue of basic world views compiled by the editor of IVP. In its fifth printing at that time!

Smith, Wilbur. *Therefore Stand.* Boston: W. A. Wilde & Co., 1945. A plea for a vigorous apologetic to again be proclaimed by the church militant. Smith was an able defender of the faith, and this book is worth buying for the footnotes alone.

Sproul, R. C. *Reasons to Believe.* Dallas: Regal Books, 1978. Sproul is thoroughly Reformed theologically and a very competent apologist. This work is a simple compilation of basic apologetical questions and answers. Sproul's formal work on apologetics, entitled *Classical Apologetics* (Grand Rapids: Zondervan, 1984), unfortunately displays how deeply he has imbibed at the founts of Calvinist presuppositional apologetics as espoused by Cornelius Van Til.

Stiller, Gunther. *Johann Sebastian Bach and Liturgical Life in Leipzig.* St. Louis: Concordia Publishing House, 1984. This book helps to explain why J. S. Bach is often called simply "The Fifth Evangelist." To fully appreciate Bach, the sensitive interpreter must understand Luther's "theology of the cross" and the centrality of that focus in the music of Bach. For example, all of Luther's approximately 40 hymns can be found in the works of Bach. In many ways the Reformation in Germany died for almost a century with the death of Bach in 1750 as pietism ran rampant. Stiller will help you to understand Bach's colossal impact on western culture as a direct outgrowth of his thorough commitment to the teachings of the Lutheran Reformation. The full collection of the works of J. S. Bach now total 171 CDs, and yet he never composed a symphony or an opera. Every church musician should sit at his feet.

Stoll, Clifford. *High Tech Heretic: Why Computers Don't Belong in the Classroom and Other Reflections by a Computer Contrarian.* New York: Doubleday, 1999. Important reading on why cyberknowledge is overvalued. Anything that is fast and free should be accepted with caution, says the author. Stoll is a founder of the Internet and sees it as having become in large part the junk food of technological discoveries. He advocates no computers in the classroom, no use of calculators until well into mastery of basic math, and a reclaiming of the fact that learning is work and not necessarily always "fun." This is a must-read for those having to deal with the "Corporate Bobs" in the church and elsewhere (see the movie *Office Space* if this does not ring a bell) who are always thinking marketing and "bottom line" and technology, rather than advocating reading old books or listening to a Bach cantata or mastering a solid catechism. Stoll's chapter on the misuse of PowerPoint presentations by pastors is worth the price of the book alone. The author calls for the renaissance of the great profession of teaching. As Stoll puts it, our society's problems are rooted "in a love affair with gizmos" and society's fascination with the lie that "information is power."

Veith, Gene Edward, Jr. *State of the Arts—From Bezalel to Mapplethorpe.* Wheaton: Crossways Books, 1991. Thorough discussion of why Christians must not abandon the arts to secularists. Veith has an excellent section on developing objective criteria for analyzing works of art and traces how a small group of people are able to sell wealthy patrons on the artistic merits of often trivial (and not uncommonly perverse) works of "art" as the role of the "artistic interpreter" has risen.

Note: Books by John Warwick Montgomery and Craig Parton can be purchased through the Canadian Institute for Law, Theology, and Public Policy located at 7203-90 Avenue in Edmonton, Alberta, Canada, T6B OP5 (www.lights.com/caninst/ or e-mail at: ciltpp@cs.com).

NOTES

INTRODUCTION

1. See John Warwick Montgomery's excellent chapter entitled "Luther and the Rise of Modern Science" in the work *In Defense of Martin Luther* (Milwaukee: Northwestern Publishing House, 1970), pp. 88–112, as well as Montgomery's fascinating introductory essay on Lutheranism, astronomy, astrology, and alchemy found in his two-volume work entitled *Cross and Crucible,* vol. 1 (The Hague: Martinus Nijhoff, 1973). In addition, Werner Elert puts it well when he says, "If the teaching of Copernicus was fostered at the universities at all, this took place in the domain of Lutheranism." *The Structure of Lutheranism,* vol. 1, trans. Walter A. Hansen (St. Louis: Concordia Publishing House, 1962), p. 426.

2. The term *evangelical* comes from the Greek word *evangellion,* or *evangel.* It simply means "Good News," or in the common English contraction, "Gospel." The Lutherans in sixteenth-century Germany were originally called "Evangelicals" because of their primary emphasis on Christ's atoning death and resurrection. In modern America by contrast, *Evangelical* denotes a wide spectrum of conservative Protestant denominations, generally Calvinist or Arminian in theology.

3. See Vladimir Lossky, *Mystical Theology of the Eastern Church* (Crestwood, NY: St. Vladimir's Seminary Press, 1972), p. 26.

4. Both Francois Wendel and Alistair McGrath refuse to characterize Calvin as having one central theological focus. Both, however, agree that the doctrine of justification is *not* any more central than the sovereignty of God, predestination, or the role of the Law. Francois Wendel, *Calvin: Origins and Development of His Religious Thought* (Grand Rapids: Baker Books, 1950), p. 358; Alistair McGrath, *A Life of John Calvin* (London: Blackwell Publishers, 1990), p. 165.

CHAPTER 1

1. Mary Baker Eddy's mind-science cult, a nineteenth-century version of ancient first-century Gnosticism. Gnosticism was scathingly addressed by the apostle John in 1 John 4:1–3. It taught that God didn't care much for matter—the "spirit" was what really counted. John dealt this heresy the definitive refutation by showing that it ultimately denied the incarnation and the full and essential humanity of God the Son. See Harold O. J. Brown, *Heresies: The Image of Christ in the Mirror of Heresy and Orthodoxy from the Apostles to the Present* (Garden City, New York: Doubleday & Co., Inc., 1984), pp. 38–69; see also the disturbing discussion of modern-day Evangelical teachings on the so-called "spiritual" or "higher" life and their origins in thoroughly Gnostic views of the physical world as presented in Michael Horton's trenchant article "The New Gnosticism," *Modern Reformation* (July/August 1995): pp. 4–12.

2. See Craig Parton, "From Arrowhead to Augsburg: Bill Bright in the Light of the Lutheran Confessions," *Reformation & Revival Journal* 5, no. 1 (Winter 1996): pp. 81–94.

3. The three ladders of ascent for medieval monks were rationalism, mysticism, and legalism (perhaps modern equivalents are dead orthodoxy, the charismatic movement, and fundamentalism). All have a common theme, since all are in essence an effort to strive to reach God "from beneath." See Anders Nygren's brilliant treatment of the division between revealed religion and all attempts to reach God from the bottom up. *Agape and Eros* (London: SPCK Press, 1953), pp. 621 ff.

CHAPTER 2

1. For a series of marvelous articles defending various aspects of Christian truth done by legally trained minds through the centuries, see John Warwick Montgomery, ed., *Jurisprudence: A Book of Readings* (Strasbourg, France: International Scholarly Publishers, 1974). See also Ross Clifford, "Leading Lawyers' Case for Christianity" (Edmonton, Alberta: Canadian Institute for Law, Theology, and Public Policy, 1996).

2. Craig Parton, "Richard Whately: A Man for All Seasons" (Edmonton, Alberta: Canadian Institute for Law, Theology, and Public Policy, 1997).

3. See Craig Parton, "The New White-Wine Pietists," *Logia: A Journal of Lutheran Theology* 6, no. 1 (Epiphany 1997): pp. 33–36.

4. The development of pasteurized grape juice by Thomas Welch as a substitute for Communion wine is well documented. Welch, a pietistic, temperance-minded nineteenth-century Methodist, pioneered what is today a $650 million-a-year grape juice business, a business that benefited directly from Protestant churches in the nineteenth century caught up in the burgeoning temperance movement. Welch's motivation in pasteurizing grape juice was utterly clear—he sought the end of the "scandal" of serving alcohol in the church. Perhaps just as fascinating, at the same time there began the first theological attempts at claiming that wine was not used in Communion in the New Testament and that Jesus was actually a teetotaler. See Richard Ostling, "Wine or Grape Juice: A Communion Conundrum," Associated Press article, *Salt Lake Tribune,* 18 May, 2002; William Chazanof, *Welch's Grape Juice: From Corporation to Cooperative* (New York: Syracuse University Press, 1977); Betty O'Brien, "The Lord's Supper: Traditional Cup or Innovative Cups of Individuality," *Methodist History* 32, no. 2 (January 1994): pp. 79–98.

5. Paul Zietlow has done an excellent analysis of Luther's arguments concerning infant Baptism, arranged by the categories of biblical, theological, and historical considerations. Zietlow and others make plain that the Baptism of infants was clearly the universal practice of the Christian church from the first century until the rise of the sixteenth-century Anabaptists in response to Luther. Paul H. Zietlow, "Martin Luther's Arguments for Infant Baptism," *Concordia Journal* 20, no. 2 (April 1994): pp. 147–171; See also the definitive treatment of this topic by Jere-

mias, where he states: "*Delay of baptism in the case of Christian children was wholly unknown in the primitive Church.* It is not until the year 329–30 that we have certain evidence of a case of Christian parents letting their children grow up unbaptized" (emphasis in the original). Joachim Jeremias, *Infant Baptism in the First Four Centuries* (London: SCM Press, 1960), p. 56.

6. Martin Chemnitz, *The Lord's Supper* (St. Louis: Concordia Publishing House, 1979). Chemnitz was particularly distressing to read for me as a lawyer because he argues that in light of Christ's impending death, He was not likely to speak ambiguously or figuratively but plainly and literally. This matched up perfectly with the legal evidential concept of the "dying declaration" and the presumption in the law that someone anticipating death is telling the truth and will speak plainly and literally. Both California and federal law have statutory provisions making dying declarations admissible as against a hearsay objection. California Evidence Code Section 1242 and Federal Rule of Evidence Section 804 (b) (2). For those searching for serious biblical analysis in this area, I strongly suggest the work of Hermann Sasse. See especially, Hermann Sasse, *This Is My Body: Luther's Contention for the Real Presence in the Sacrament of the Altar* (Adelaide, South Australia: Openbook Publishers, 1977). This volume has a reconstruction based on primary source documents of the actual dialogue between Luther and the Swiss reformer Zwingli at the Marbourg Colloquy in 1528 on the meaning of Christ's words "this is my body" in the institution of the Lord's Supper.

CHAPTER 3

1. *Lutheran Worship* (St. Louis: Concordia Publishing House, 1982), p. 158.

2. See Arthur Just, "Structure, Culture, and Theology in Lutheran Liturgy," in *Worship in the Lutheran Congregation: The '90s and Beyond,* Concordia Seminary Monograph Series—Symposium Papers, no.1 (St. Louis: Concordia Seminary, 1992): pp. 9–31. For an excellent discussion of the basic Lutheran service and the biblical passages that support its components, see John T. Pless, "A Narrative Commentary on the Divine Service" (Minneapolis: Lutheran Student Fellowship, University of Minnesota, 1994) found in Appendix A.

3. For further analysis of the role of architecture, the arts, and decorum and reverence in Christian worship, see Wayne Schmidt, "The Setting of the Liturgy and the Decorum of Its Leaders," in *Lutheran Worship: History and Practice,* ed. Fred L. Precht (St. Louis: Concordia Publishing House, 1993), pp. 175–219.

4. F. Bente, *Historical Introductions to the Book of Concord* (St. Louis: Concordia Publishing House, 1965), p. 76.

5. Two excellent works on the Lutheran doctrine of sanctification are by Harold Senkbeil and Adolf Koberle. Senkbeil analyzes the Lutheran doctrine of sanctification using the writings of Charles Swindoll as his foil. Koberle's work (a modern reprint is herein cited) is the critical historical and theological work establishing that the Gospel is actually the first and last word for the doctrines of

justification and sanctification. See Harold Senkbeil, *Sanctification: Christ in Action* (Milwaukee: Northwestern Publishing House, 1992) and Adolf Koberle, *The Quest for Holiness* (Evansville: Ballast Press, 1996).

6. See Donald Deffner's article on the historical background to confirmation found in *Lutheran Worship: History and Practice*, ed. Fred L. Precht, pp. 387–400.

7. The catechesis described here is the traditional Lutheran method. This may vary in some congregations according to local custom. In the Lutheran system, confirmation does not make one a member of the church. Baptism does. That membership through Baptism is reaffirmed at confirmation—and indeed often throughout one's Christian life in confession and absolution and in making the sign of the holy cross at appropriate times. So an adult convert to the Christian faith takes catechesis toward the Baptism he is about to receive, whereas a baptized believer like my daughter takes catechesis in relationship to the Baptism she has received. Eventually my wife and I also took instruction prior to being received into membership in the Lutheran church and being admitted to the Lord's Table.

CHAPTER 4

1. See Arthur C. Cochrane, "The Act of Confession-Confessing," (in *Formula of Concord: Quadricentennial Essays) The Sixteenth Century Journal* 8, no. 4 (1977): pp. 61–83. Cochrane sets out why confessing the faith necessarily involves condemning false doctrine and heresy also.

2. Evangelicals generally have very little interest in theological history. Thus, the fact that current Evangelical teaching on the premillenial rapture of the church has its roots in the teaching of John Nelson Darby (1800–82) in the mid-nineteenth century is largely unknown. Similarly, Evangelicals ignore the fact that infant Baptism was the uniform historic practice of the church until the sixteenth-century Anabaptist reaction to the Lutheran Reformation.

3. The subject of when Luther actually made his "Reformation breakthrough" is still a subject of scholarly debate. James Kiecker points out that whether Luther was addressing the issue of the Lord's Supper, penance and confession, or man's will and whether it was free or enslaved, the primary issue at stake was the Gospel and how it comes to the sinner. See James G. Kiecker, *Martin Luther and the Long Reformation* (Milwaukee: Northwestern Publishing House, 1992), pp. 134 ff. and also Alister McGrath, Luther's Theology of the Cross: Martin Luther's Theological Breakthrough (Oxford: Blackwell, 1995).

4. There is no question that Luther had a God-given talent for clarity and bluntness. He called the papal bull that excommunicated him "execrable" and its author—the pope—the "Antichrist." Luther and his students actually burned the letter of excommunication along with a collection of scholastic writings. For the whole story, unedited and with the polemical—and utterly hilarious—woodcuts done during the time, see the standard source on the reformer by the late Yale historian Roland Bainton, *Here I Stand: A Life of Martin Luther* (New York: Abingdon-Cokesbury Press, 1950), pp. 156–66. Also recommended are Martin Brecht,

Martin Luther: His Road to Reformation (Philadelphia: Fortress, 1985) and James M. Kittelson, *Luther the Reformer: The Story of the Man and His Career* (Minneapolis: Augsburg, 1986).

5. It is worth noting that Luther had achieved the highest academic degrees possible at the time—a Master of Arts from Erfurt (1507) and a Doctor of Theology from Wittenberg (1512). It was his solemn oath at becoming a doctor (teacher) in service to the church for the sake of Christ and His Word that convinced Luther of the necessity to speak up against the abuses of the pope. The confessions of the Lutheran Reformation were the work of the best academic minds of the day. Some of these were the renowned Greek scholar and professor of medicine, astronomy, mathematics, and philosophy—Philip Melanchthon (a professor at age 21 at the University of Wittenberg), Martin Chemnitz (whose four-volume systematic refutation of the Catholic Reformation doctrinally formalized at the Council of Trent is unsurpassed and who is known as "the second Martin, without whom the first would not be known"), and David Chytraeus (one of the authors of the "Formula of Concord" and professor at the University of Rostock). Lutheranism's origin within the context of the university has profound implications for a renewal of Lutheran mission work on the academic campus. Thinking Christians find kindred spirits among the Lutheran confessors of the sixteenth century.

6. That this is no mere academic distinction is pointed out well by Sasse where he describes how churches that have taken the route of nullifying the authority of their confessions have quickly gone on to nullifying the authority of Holy Scripture. See Hermann Sasse, "Quatenus or Quia?" in *The Lonely Way: Essays and Letters 1927–1939* (St. Louis: Concordia Publishing House, 2001).

7. The purpose, says Robert Kolb, of *The Book of Concord* was to have a *corpus doctrinae* (body of doctrine) in order to "give proper form and an organized summary of the teaching of the Scriptures, which had been divinely restored through Luther's ministry, as this teaching had been expressed in the creeds tested by the church. Such a body of teaching would benefit the church, for it would provide a norm or standard of judgment so that cleverly disguised interpretations and obfuscations of the Biblical text could be rejected. If such standards are not in place in the church, Chemnitz observed, pure teaching will disappear." Robert Kolb, *Confessing the Faith: Reformers Define the Church, 1530–1580* (St. Louis: Concordia Publishing House, 1991), p. 119.

8. David P. Scaer, "All Theology Is Christology," *Modern Reformation* 8, no. 5 (September–October 1999): pp. 28–32.

9. Ewald Plass, *What Luther Says: An Anthology* (St. Louis: Concordia Publishing House, 1959), vol. 1, sec. 208, p. 70. For those with access to the American edition of Luther's Works published by Concordia, see vol. 35, p. 132.

10. Winthrop Hudson, *Religion in America* (New York: Scribners, 1965), p. 176. Mark A. Noll, professor of history at Wheaton College and not a Lutheran, has also written a remarkable piece on the historic opportunity of the Lutheran church to save Evangelicalism from total collapse. See his article entitled "The

Lutheran Difference," in *First Things: A Journal of Religion and Public Life,* no. 20 (February 1992): pp. 31–40.

11. John Warwick Montgomery, "The Holy Spirit and the Defense of the Faith," *Bibliotheca Sacra, A Journal of the Dallas Theological School* 154, no. 616 (October–December, 1997): pp. 387–95.

CHAPTER 5

1. One thinks immediately of those in the Calvinist camp, such as Cornelius Van Til, Alvin Platinga, and John Frame, who present largely philosophical and presuppositional apologetical approaches. R. C. Sproul, however, has taken a courageous stand vis-à-vis Van Til. Sproul has championed a call to return to evidential apologetics and sees it in no way as contradictory to Calvinism. See Sproul's *Classical Apologetics* (Grand Rapids: Zondervan Publishing House, 1984). For the best critique of Van Til's rigid Calvinist presuppositional apologetic, see John Montgomery, *Faith Founded on Fact: Essays in Evidential Apologetics* (Nashville: Thomas Nelson Publishers, 1978), especially pp. 107–27 for his article "Once Upon an Apriori: Van Til in Light of Three Fables."

2. See Luther's explanation of the Third Article of the Apostles' Creed.

3. Interestingly, Scripture says that "even the demons believe that—and shudder" (James 2:19). The demons correctly comprehend facts (i.e., that God exists) and even interpret them correctly (they shudder before His holiness). This does not mean, however, that the demons have a saving faith.

4. Luther's explanation of the First Article of the Creed says that God the Father has given us "[our] reason and all [our] senses, and still takes care of them."

5. John Montgomery, "Lutheranism and the Defense of the Christian Faith," *Lutheran Synod Quarterly* 9, no. 1 (Fall, 1970): pp. 1–56.

6. See Pinchas Lapide, *The Resurrection of Jesus: A Jewish Perspective* (Minneapolis: Augsburg, 1983). Lapide, a Jewish New Testament scholar, agrees that Jesus in fact rose from the dead, but he argues that life after death is part of the Jewish "faith experience" and is separate from the issue of Jesus' Messiahship.

7. In the Creed we say, "I believe," not "I see." Pilate saw but did not believe.

8. New York: Harper, 1931.

9. Jean Guitton, *Journal, 1952–55* (Paris: Librairie Plon, 1959), pp. 19–21.

10. Karl Barth, *Anselm: Quaerens Intellectum: Anselm's Proof of the Existence of God in the Context of His Theological Scheme,* trans. I. W. Robertson (Richmond, VA: John Knox Press, 1960), pp. 71, 170.

11. Rudolph Bultmann, *The Presence of Eternity: History and Eschatology,* The Gifford Lectures 1955 (Harper & Row: New York, 1957), p. 155. Just as Albert Schweitzer did in *The Quest of the Historical Jesus,* Bultmann tears the heart of Christian faith out by asserting that Jesus erred in believing that His death would usher in the kingdom of God and the eschatological end of the age. Anti-Christian philosopher Walter Kaufmann puts it well in analyzing Bultmann's logic: "If

first-rate scholars like Rudolf Bultmann and Albert Schweitzer are right that Jesus was mistaken about the central tenet and premise of his message, why should not this undermine our confidence in his authority?" Walter Kaufmann, *Critique of Religion and Philosophy* (New York: Harper & Row, 1958), p. 153.

12. For a fascinating account of one of Bultmann's brightest students, her ultimate rejection of Bultmann's method, and her discovery of a Christ ever willing to save, see Eta Linnemann, *Historical Criticism of the Bible: Methodology or Ideology? Reflections of a Bultmannian Turned Evangelical,* trans. Robert Yarbrough (Grand Rapids: Baker Books, 1990). In that work you find the following remarkable *mea maxima culpa:* "I regard everything that I taught and wrote before I entrusted my life to Jesus as refuse. I wish to use this opportunity to mention that I have pitched my two books *Gleichnisse Jesu. . .* and *Studien zur Passionsgeschichte,* along with my contributions to journals, anthologies, and *Festschriften.* Whatever of these writings I had in my possession I threw into the trash with my own hands in 1978. I ask you sincerely to do the same thing with any of them you may have on your own bookshelf" (p. 20).

13. The best interpretation of the facts will not, as David Hume did, disregard data a priori because it points to the supernatural and argues for the miraculous. As any good trial lawyer knows, facts arbitrate competing interpretations of those facts. For a superb destruction of Hume's argument against the miraculous, read the work of the nineteenth-century Anglican apologist Richard Whately, who almost single-handedly decimated Hume by applying Hume's flawed method of historical analysis to another controversial figure—Napoléon Bonaparte. Whately, tongue-in-cheek, concluded that Hume's method of doubting any unusual and unrepeatable historical events resulted in the conclusion that Napoléon never existed. Whately wrote this while Napoléon was still alive on the Island of Elba! See Parton, *Richard Whately.*

14. The medieval ladders of ascent attempted by Luther and found to be dead ends.

15. R. C. H. Lenski, *Interpretation of the Acts of the Apostles* (Columbus, Ohio: The Wartburg Press, 1944), pp. 711–13.

16. Richard Longenecker, *Paul, Apostle of Liberty* (New York: Harper, 1964), p. 230. For a particularly brilliant analysis of the apostle Paul's apologetical skill among the Stoic and Epicurean philosophers on Mars Hill, see Wilbur Smith, *Therefore Stand: A Plea for a Vigorous Apologetic in this Critical Hour of the Christian Faith* (Boston: W. A. Wilde Co., 1950), pp. 246–71. Smith makes plain that the comparison between the gnostic and cultic panoply of gods in Athens and the plethora of isms, cults, and false religions in our own day is simply chilling.

17. See discussion by eminent Lutheran theologians Siegbert W. Becker in *The Foolishness of God: The Place of Reason in the Theology of Martin Luther* (Milwaukee: Northwestern Publishing House, 1982), p. 148, and J. T. Mueller in *Christian Dogmatics* (St. Louis: Concordia Publishing House, 1934), p. 71. Despite their otherwise excellent work, both Becker and Mueller unfortunately reduce evangelism and apologetics to preaching at unbelievers rather than reasoning with them.

18. Montgomery, *Faith Founded on Fact,* p. 38.

19. Arthur Koestler et al., The God That Failed, ed. Richard H. Crossman (New York: Books for Libraries, 1949).

20. Arthur Koestler, *The Lotus and the Robot* (New York: Harper & Row, 1960), pp. 273–74. Koestler's disillusionment comes to a final terminus when he discovers that Buddhism finds Hitler's acts only "silly" while Christianity confronts them as clear "evil." Eastern mysticism became for Koestler an odorless and tasteless nerve gas devoid of moral strength and the ability to confront evil and human wretchedness. Tragically, Koestler and his wife committed mutual suicide.

21. Anthony Flew, "Theology and Falsification," *New Essays in Philosophical Theology,* ed. Anthony Flew and Alasdair MacIntyre (London: SCM Press, 1955), p. 96.

22. WA, vol. 36, pp. 61 ff. (sermon of 6 January, 1532, on Micah 5:1), cited in Ewald Plass, *What Luther Says,* p. 552.

23. B. A. Garrish, *Grace and Reason* (Oxford: Clarendon Press, 1962), pp. 72–73 ("For the Kingdom of Human Reason must be separated as far as possible from the Spiritual Kingdom."); R. H. Fischer, "A Reasonable Luther," in *Reformation Studies: Essays in Honor of Roland H. Bainton,* ed. F. H. Littell (Richmond, Va.: John Knox, 1962), pp. 30–45, especially p. 39 ("Such insights [reason, experience, common sense] operate in what would later be called the phenomenal realm; they do not penetrate the noumenal.").

24. See also George W. Forell, *Faith Active in Love* (Minneapolis: Augsburg Press, 1959), pp. 121, 149.

25. John Warwick Montgomery, "Luther and Science," *Transactions of the Royal Society of Canada,* 4th ser., 1 (1963), pp. 251–70. See also Montgomery's article on the topic found in *In Defense of Martin Luther* (Milwaukee: Northwestern Publishing House, 1970), pp. 88–112.

26. The list is impressive, including Chemnitz, Heerbrand, Hunnius, Hafenreffer, Gerhard, Andreae, Calov, Quenstedt, Baier, and Hollaz. These dogmaticians and their apologetical contributions are discussed in detail in Montgomery's "Lutheran Theology and the Defense of Biblical Faith," *Lutheran Synod Quarterly* 9, no. 1 (Fall 1970), pp. 1–56; see also J. Pelikan, "Natural Theology in David Hollaz," *Concordia Theological Monthly* 15 (1947): pp. 253–63. Natural theology, or natural revelation as commonly understood, deals with what can be learned about God from the nature of the world. At its best, natural theology does not go so far as Christ and the cross.

CHAPTER 6

1. Kai Nielsen, "Can Faith Validate God-Talk?" in *New Theology No. 1,* ed. Frederick Ferre, *Language, Logic and God* (New York: Harper, 1961), pp. 94–104.

2. For the English edition see Hugo Grotius, *On the Truth of the Christian Religion* (London: William Baynes & Son, 1825) reprinted in part in Montgomery, ed., *Jurisprudence: A Book of Readings,* pp. 319–31.

3. Simon Greenleaf, *The Testimony of the Evangelists: The Gospels Examined by the Rules of Evidence* (New York: J. C. & Co., 1874; Grand Rapids: Kregel, 1995).

4. Lord Hailsham, *The Door Wherein I Went* (London: Collins, 1975). Hailsham, until his death in 2001, was considered one of the leading legal luminaries in all of England.

5. Norman Anderson, *The Evidence for the Resurrection of Jesus Christ* (London: Inter-Varsity Press, 1966); *Christianity: The Witness of History* (Oxford: Tyndale Press, 1969); *Christianity and Comparative Religion* (London: Inter-Varsity Press, 1970).

6. Jacques Ellul, *Theological Foundation of Law,* trans. Marguerite Wieser (New York: Seabury Press, 1969). Ellul's trenchant analysis of technological culture and the utter dehumanizing of man in the twentieth century is always worthy of reflection. Unfortunately, Ellul is thoroughly neoorthodox in theological orientation and a devout Barthian. Therefore it is with sadness that one reads in Ellul's autobiography that he has ended up with a doctrine of universal salvation. See Jacques Ellul, *What I Believe,* trans. Geoffrey W. Bromiley (Grand Rapids: Eeerdmans, 1989), pp. 188 ff.

7. Many of Montgomery's books and debates are available through the Canadian Institute for Law, Theology, and Public Policy (Institut canadien de droit, theologie et politiques publiques) in Edmonton, Alberta, Canada (www.ciltpp.com). Professor Montgomery is the Director of the International Academy of Apologetics, Evangelism and Human Rights located in Strasbourg, France (www.trinitysem.edu/catalog/intacad.html). Dr. Montgomery and the author are members of the permanent faculty of the Academy, where we teach in the areas of legal, historical, philosophical, literary, and scientific apologetics each summer. Dr. Montgomery's most recent contribution to legal apologetics is his book *Christ Our Advocate: Studies in Polemical Theology, Jurisprudence and Canon Law* (Bonn: Culture & Science Publishers, 2002).

8. Stephen E. Toulmin, *The Uses of Argument* (Cambridge: Cambridge University Press, 1958), p. 7. Says Toulmin: "So let us forget about psychology, sociology, technology and mathematics, ignore the echoes of structural engineering and *collage* in the words "grounds" and "backing," and take as our model the discipline of jurisprudence. Logic (we may say) is generalized jurisprudence. Arguments can be compared with lawsuits, and the claims we make and argue for in extra-legal contexts with claims made in the courts, while the cases we present in making good each kind of claim can be compared with each other."

9. Dr. Adler, a self-described pagan for most of his life, converted to Christianity in 1984 and was baptized by an Episcopalian priest on April 21 of that year (see his account in Chapter 9 of his second autobiography *A Second Look in the Rearview Mirror: Further Autobiographical Reflections of a Philosopher at Large* [St. Martin's Press, 1994]. In December of 1999 he converted to Roman Catholicism (radicalacademy.com/adlerbio.htm).

10. Mortimer J. Adler, *How to Think about God* (New York: Macmillan Press,

1980), p. 150. Adler, the eminent University of Chicago philosopher, is dealing here with the general existence of God, a question traditionally in the realm of natural theology. But note that Adler, born a Jew, did not stop here. For Adler, natural revelation was only a prelude to special revelation.

11. Federal Civil Jury Instruction 72.01 defines "preponderance of evidence" as the clear burden put upon the plaintiff in any civil action (in the case of evangelism, the effective Christian advocate clearly is the plaintiff who is going for a verdict). The judge in a Federal civil jury trial will instruct as follows on the issue of the burden of proof: "a preponderance of the evidence in the case means such evidence as, when considered and compared with that opposed to it, has more convincing force, and produces in your minds belief that what is sought to be proved is more likely true than not true. *This rule does not, of course, require proof to an absolute certainty, since proof to an absolute certainty is seldom possible in any case"* (emphasis added).

CHAPTER 7

1. Elert calls all aspects of Christ's ministry that reveal man's sin as His *opus alienum*. The "proper work" of Christ *(opus proprium)* is that which issues from the mercy of God and is nothing less than the Gospel itself. It is the Gospel, the Good News of the forgiveness of sins won on the cross and now freely offered to repentant mankind, that sets Christianity apart from all other religions that must be religions of law. Werner Elert, *The Structure of Lutheranism,* vol. 1 (St. Louis: Concordia Publishing House, 1962), p. 212, citing Luther.

2. Dr. Stroll's entire address on this occasion, entitled "Did Jesus Really Exist?", is reprinted (with his own corrections) as Appendix A in John Warwick Montgomery's book *Where Is History Going? A Christian Response to Secular Philosophies of History* (Minneapolis: Bethany Publishers, 1969).

3. C. S. Lewis, *Christian Reflections* (Grand Rapids: Eerdmans, 1967), pp. 158–60.

4. John A. T. Robinson, *Redating the New Testament* (London: SCM Press, 1976), pp. 351–52.

5. William Albright, *Recent Discoveries in Bible Lands* (New York: Funk and Wagnalls, 1955), p. 136. For a complete discussion of the manuscript documentation for the Gospels, see J. P. Moreland, *Scaling the Secular City: A Defense of Christianity* (Grand Rapids: Baker Books, 1987), especially chapter 5, "The Historicity of the New Testament." In addition, the entire subject of the manuscript authority for the New Testament is handled in Montgomery's magnum opus, *Tractatus Logico-Theologicus* (Bonn: Culture & Science Publishers, 2002), especially chapter 3, which covers the following: "Proposition: Historical, jurisprudential and scientific standards of evidence offer the touchstone for resolving the religious predicament by establishing the truth claims of Christian proclamation."

6. F. F. Bruce, *The New Testament Documents: Are They Reliable?* (Grand Rapids: Eerdmans, 1987), pp. 16–17; for the paucity of manuscript evidence concerning

Catallus see G. Lee, ed., *Catullus: The Complete Poems* (Oxford: Oxford University Press, 1989), pp. ix–xiv and L. D. Reynolds and N. G. Wilson, *Scribes and Scholars: A Guide to the Transmission of Greek and Latin Literature,* 3rd ed. (Oxford: Clarendon Press, 1968). Reynolds and Wilson note: "One cannot consider these facts without marveling at the slenderness of the thread on which the fate of the Latin classics hung. In the case of many texts a single copy survived into the Carolingian period, and often a battered one at that. When the great period of the revival was over, some of the great works of Latin literature were still but a single manuscript on a single shelf. The slightest accident could still have robbed us of some of our most precious texts, of Catullus and Propertius, Petronius or Tacitus" (pp. 101–2).

7. Frederick G. Kenyon, *Handbook to the Textual Criticism of the New Testament,* 2nd ed. (London: Macmillan, 1912), p. 5. For confirmation of all of these dates, along with the addition of other works of antiquity in comparison to the Gospel manuscripts, see F. W. Hall, "MS. Authorities for the Text of the Chief Classical Writers," in *Companion to Classical Texts* (Oxford: Clarendon Press, 1913), pp. 199 ff.

8. Frederick G. Kenyon, *The Bible and Archaeology* (New York: Harper, 1940), pp. 288–89 (emphasis in the original). I have not even presented the argument from the recent papyrus fragment found on Christmas Eve in 1994 sitting on a shelf in a jar at Magdalen College in Oxford. Papyrologist Carsten Thiede and Matthew D'Ancona argue that this fragment corroborates that Matthew wrote the Gospel bearing his name, that he wrote it within a generation of Jesus' death, that the Gospels are historically accurate, and that they come essentially contemporaneously with the events they record. See Thiede and D'Ancona, *Eyewitness to Jesus: Amazing New Manuscript Evidence About the Origin of the Gospels* (New York: Doubleday, 1996).

9. This exception to the hearsay rule is contained in California and federal law (California Evidence Code Section 1331 and Federal Rule of Evidence 803[16]). Professor Greenleaf surveyed the common law on the topic at the time and found that it provided that ancient documents are admissible as competent evidence if they are "fair on their face" (i.e., show no evidence of tampering) and have been maintained in "reasonable custody" (preserved in a manner and in a place consistent with their content). Greenleaf concludes that the New Testament Gospels would be admissible under this exception to the hearsay rule. Greenleaf, *The Testimony of the Evangelists,* pp. 16 ff. The burden of proof in a court of law then shifts to the critic to establish that the documents are unreliable, forgeries, or contain factual inaccuracies.

10. Hailsham, *The Door Wherein I Went,* pp. 32–33. The theological and apologetical material in Hailsham's autobiography have been photolithographically reproduced in *The Simon Greenleaf Law Review* 4 (1984–85): pp. 1–67.

11. We must remember that we ascribe the conclusion of inerrancy to the documentary *autographs* only and not to copies, though, as shown, our copies are uniquely reliable, and that we hold to inerrancy in general chiefly because He who died an atoning death on Calvary's cross, and verified His claims by His res-

urrection, held to such a view. "The Scripture cannot be broken" (John 10:35). This is why the so-called "King James only" proponents are misguided when they argue for the sole use of a certain translation. Inerrancy is not, and cannot be, connected to a translation, even though our translations, though derivative, are faithful representations of the originals. As for why this is not an asylum of ignorance nor an unfalsifiable position (i.e., "what we believe in is true, it just doesn't exist, and so you can't disprove it"), see Gleason Archer's excellent article entitled "The Importance of Biblical Inerrancy" found in his *Encyclopedia of Bible Difficulties* (Grand Rapids: Zondervan Publishing House, 1982), pp. 19–44; see also John Warwick Montgomery, ed., *God's Inerrant Word: An International Symposium on the Trustworthiness of Scripture,* (Minneapolis: Bethany Publishing House, 1974) and Montgomery's *Crisis in Lutheran Theology,* 2d ed., 2 vols. (Minneapolis: Bethany Publishing House, 1973). One hastens to note that we have not even attempted to present the case for establishing the life and death of Christ using *nonbiblical* and pagan sources, an approach that has been fruitfully pursued by C. R. Haines, Lord Hailsham (see *The Door Wherein I Went*), and Gary Habermas. See Haines, *Heathen Contact with Christianity During Its First Century and a Half: Being All References to Christianity Recorded in Pagan Writings During That Period* (Cambridge: Deighton, Bell, 1923) and Habermas, *Ancient Evidence for the Life of Jesus* (Nashville: Thomas Nelson Publishers, 1984) (analyzing 39 ancient sources establishing 110 facts concerning the life, teachings, death, and resurrection of Christ—pp. 169 ff.).

12. That the apostolic witnesses claim to have been eyewitnesses to these remarkable statements and that Jesus Christ is alleged to have made Himself equal to God and able to forgive sins is made palpably clear through the New Testament writings (see 2 Peter 1:16–18; John 1:1; 1 John 1:1; John 8:58; John 20:27–28; John 8:24; Luke 5:18–24).

13. Alan Saltzman, "Criminal Law: How to Expose Perjury Through Cross-Examination," *Los Angeles Daily Journal,* 4 November 1982.

14. Patrick L. McCloskey and Ronald L. Schoenberg, *Criminal Law Advocacy,* vol. 5 (New York: Matthew Bender, 1984), para. 12.01[b]. The application of this test to the New Testament writers is dealt with extensively, and brilliantly, by John Warwick Montgomery in *Human Rights and Human Dignity* (Grand Rapids: Zondervan Publishing, 1986), pp. 140 ff.

15. Acts 1:3 and Acts 26:25–26. The entire exchange in verses 24–29 shows how apologetically adept, and evangelistically sensitive, the apostle was when encountering paganism (contrast this with the attitude of many Christians that can be summarized by the phrase "Losing an argument? Yell louder."). Though Festus accuses Paul of insanity, the apostle does not retaliate with slander or similar *ad hominem* argument but instead points outside himself to the objectivity of the cross and the resurrection—the central verities of the Christian claim ("these things did not happen in a corner"). Paul then shifts his appeal and apologetic to King Agrippa and plays off of Agrippa's knowledge and apparent belief in the Old Testament Jewish prophets to move the conversation along to a confrontation with the crucified and risen Savior.

16. Hugo Grotius, *De Veritata Religiones Christianae* ("On the Truth of the Christian Religion"), trans. John Clarke (London: William Baynes, 1825), bk. 2, sec. 6 ("The resurrection of Christ proved from credible testimony"), pp. 85–88. Critical portions of Grotius's work have been reprinted in Montgomery, *Jurisprudence: A Book of Readings,* pp. 327–30.

17. See, for example, John 8:44 (KJV), where Jesus explicitly teaches that lying is of the devil, "who was a liar from the beginning."

18. "People just do not see things in an identical way when their positions and chances for observation vary. [If so,] the case is a frame-up"—F. Lee Bailey and Henry B. Rothblatt, *Fundamentals of Criminal Advocacy* (San Francisco: Bancroft-Whitney, 1974), para. 500, p. 4.

19. John Warwick Montgomery, "The Jury Returns: A Juridical Defense of Christianity," in *Evidence for Faith: Deciding the God Question,* ed. J. W. Montgomery (Dallas: Probe Books, 1991), p. 325.

20. A. Jaubert, *La Date de la Cene. Calendrier biblique et liturgie chretienne* (Paris: Gabalda, 1957). Jaubert's discovery is handled in detail by John Warwick Montgomery in "The Fourth Gospel Yesterday and Today," *Concordia Theological Monthly,* 34 (April 1963): pp. 206 ff. See also F. F. Bruce, "Archaeological Confirmation of the New Testament," in *Revelation and the Bible,* ed. Carl F. H. Henry (Grand Rapids: Baker Book House, 1958), pp. 319 ff. In addition, Josh McDowell has a very useful chapter concerning archaeological confirmation of biblical references in *Evidence That Demands a Verdict: Historical Evidences for the Christian Faith* (Arrowhead Springs: Here's Life Publishers, 1972), pp. 68–76.

21. Richard A. Givens, *Advocacy* (New York: McGraw-Hill, 1980), p. 12, emphasis added. This is clearly one reason O. J. Simpson's civil case ended in a verdict of liability while he was acquitted in the criminal matter. Simpson's lawyers in the criminal action knew the perils of having their client testify and wisely invoked the constitutional protection against self-incrimination.

22. Greenleaf, *The Testimony of the Evangelists,* pp. 31 et seq.

23. F. F. Bruce, *The New Testament Documents,* n. 15, pp. 45–46.

CHAPTER 8

1. Sir Arthur Conan Doyle, "The Sign of Four," in *The Complete Sherlock Holmes* (New York: Barnes & Noble, 1992), p. 11.

2. Matthew 12:38–40; 16:4; Luke 11:29; John 2:18–22. While I have not presented the medical evidence establishing the death of Christ, competent medical professionals have addressed the question in detail. The result has been the most solid affirmation legally possible of the historical details presented by the New Testament record as to the crucifixion and death of Christ. See William D. Edwards, M.D. et. al., "The Physical Death of Jesus Christ," *The Journal of the American Medical Society* 255, no. 11 (March 21, 1986): pp. 1455–63; C. Truman Davis, M.D., "The Crucifixion of Jesus: The Passion of Christ from a Medical Point of View," *Arizona Medicine* Vol. 22 (March 1965): pp. 183–87; Robert Wassenar, M.D.,

"A Physician Looks at the Suffering of Christ," *Moody Monthly* 79, no. 7 (March 1979) pp. 41–42; James H. Jewell, Jr., M.D. and Patricia A. Didden, M.D., "A Surgeon Looks at the Cross," *Voice* 58, no. 2 (March–April 1979): pp. 3–5.

3. David Hume, *An Inquiry Concerning Human Understanding,* ed. C.W. Hendel (New York: Bobbs-Merrill, 1955), sec. 10, pt. 1 p. 122 ff. ("Of Miracles"). Lewis's devastating critique of Hume is contained in *Miracles* (New York: MacMillan, 1947), see especially chapters 8 and 13.

4. John Warwick Montgomery, *The Shape of the Past,* rev. ed. (Minneapolis: Bethany Publishers, 1975), pp. 289–93.

5. Historically, therefore, it should come as little surprise that the rigorously logical scholastic theology of Thomas Aquinas was utterly mesmerized by natural law theorizing. Thomas Aquinas, *Summa Theologica,* bks. 1–2, QQ 90–97; see Elmer Gelinas, "The Natural Law According to Thomas Aquinas," *Simon Greenleaf Law Review* 2 (1982–83): pp. 13–36.

6. Frank Morrison, *Who Moved the Stone?* (London: Faber & Faber, 1944).

7. See the devastating critique of Schonfield done by Edwin M. Yamauchi in "Passover Plot or Easter Triumph?" contained in *The Gordon Review* (summer 1967): *Journal of the American Scientific Affiliation* 21 (March 1969).

8. Richard R. Lingeman writes that Von Daniken had "obtained the money [more than $130,000 in debts] by misrepresentation of his financial situation, falsifying the hotel's books to make it appear solvent. A court psychiatrist examined Von Daniken and found him a prestige-seeker, a liar and an unstable and criminal psychopath with a hysterical character, yet fully accountable for his acts." *New York Times Book Review,* 31 March 1974, p. 6.

9. See Montgomery's discussion on the role of Federal Rule of Evidence 401 dealing with relevant evidence. John Warwick Montgomery, *Human Rights and Human Dignity* (Dallas: Probe Books, 1986), p. 153.

10. See Gary Habermas and Anthony Flew, *Did Jesus Rise from the Dead? The Resurrection Debate,* ed. Terry L. Miethe (San Francisco: Harper & Row, 1987); see also the decimation of Flew's position done by John Warwick Montgomery in his article entitled "Science, Theology, and the Miraculous," contained in *Faith Founded on Fact* (Nashville: Thomas Nelson Publishers, 1978), pp. 43–73, especially p. 54.

11. Thomas Sherlock, *The Tryal of the Witnesses of the Resurrection of Jesus* (London: J. Roberts, 1729), p. 62. This work is reproduced in *Jurisprudence: A Book of Readings,* ed. Montgomery, with the pertinent quote found on p. 400.

12. Carl Gustav Jung, *Man and His Symbols* (New York: Doubleday & Co., 1964). Jung's discussion of the cross (along with that of Professor Mircea Eliade of the University of Chicago) as an archetype is fascinating even though Jung ended up holding to the position that religious belief was an entirely arbitrary and subjective decision. See Eliade's *Images & Symbols: Studies in Religious Symbolism* (New York: Sheed & Ward, 1969).

13. John 10:30; 14:8–9. See also Mark 2:5–7; 14:61–64.

14. Matthew 5 and the Sermon on the Mount; John 14–16. For a discussion of what Swedish theologian Oscar Cullman called the "gift of total recall" given to the apostles, see the articles entitled "The Canon of the New Testament" by Herman Ridderbos and "The Holy Spirit and the Scriptures" by J. Theodore Mueller contained in *Revelation and the Bible,* ed. Carl F. H. Henry (Grand Rapids: Baker Books, 1958), pp. 187–201, 265–281.

15. Raymond Surburg, "Implications of the Historico-Critical Method in Interpreting the Old Testament," in *Crisis in Lutheran Theology,* vol. 2, ed. J. W. Montgomery (Minneapolis: Bethany Publishing House, 1973), pp. 51–80.

16. Sir Arthur Conan Doyle, "A Scandal in Bohemia," in *The Complete Sherlock Holmes* (New York: Barnes & Noble, 1992), p. 163.

17. It is interesting to note that even in the supposedly "hard sciences" (e.g., chemistry) there is still a level of approximation, and even error, that can never be eliminated. "All components of the chemical measurement process have measurable error. . . . All lab data are approximations." Bruce Godfrey, president of Curtis and Tompkins Laboratories of Berkeley, California (one of the oldest, largest, and most prestigious chemical laboratories in the country), at a presentation at the Advanced Forensics and Legal Strategies conference held in San Francisco, 14 April, 2000, sponsored by the Department of Engineering of the University of Wisconsin—Madison and attended by the author.

18. Greenleaf, *The Testimony of the Evangelists,* pp. 132–33.

19. Keith Windschuttle, *The Killing of History* (New York: Simon & Schuster, 1996), pp. 2, 219 ff. Professor Windschuttle goes on to point out that "[a]n historical explanation is an inductive argument constructed out of evidence" id.

20. John Warwick Montgomery, "Legal Hermeneutics and the Interpretation of Scripture," *Premise* 2, no. 9 (19 October, 1995): p. 10.

21. Montgomery, id. (citing Eugene F.A. Klug, *"Sensus Literalis' das Wort in den Wortern, eine hermeneutische Meditation vom Verstehen der Bibel,"* *Evangelium* 12, no. 5 [December 1985]: pp. 165–75).

22. The Oxford *Concise Dictionary of Law* lists the "principles of statutory interpretation" in part in the following manner: (1) An Act must be construed as a whole, so that internal inconsistencies are avoided; (2) Words that are reasonably capable of only one meaning must be given that meaning whatever the result—this is the so-called *literal rule;* and (3) Ordinary words must be given their ordinary meanings and technical words their technical meanings, unless absurdity would result. *A Concise Dictionary of Law,* ed. Elizabeth Martin (Oxford: Oxford University Press, 1987), p. 189. A fuller treatment of these canons of evidence is found in Herbert Broom, "The Interpretation of Deeds and Written Instruments," chap. 8 in *Legal Maxims,* 9th ed., ed. W. J. Byrne (London: Sweet & Maxwell, 1924), pp. 342–44.

23. The parole evidence rule states that integrated writings cannot be added to, subtracted from, or varied by the admission of extrinsic evidence of prior or contemporaneous oral or written agreements. The extrinsic evidence is admissible

only to *clarify* or *explain* the integrated writing, but never to *contradict* the writing. See Uniform Commercial Code, sec. 2-202. The California rule is embodied in California Code of Civil Procedure Section 1856 (a). This would destroy, for example, the Roman doctrine of Mary as Co-Redemptrix with Christ, her Son, since this flatly contradicts 1 Timothy 2:5.

CHAPTER 9

1. William James, *The Varieties of Religious Experience: A Study in Human Nature* (London: Longmans, Green, and Co., 1907).

2. "The tough-minded and the tender-minded, as William James described them so brilliantly, are perennial types, perennially antagonistic. . . . Respect for the facts of experience, open-mindedness, an experimental trial-and-error attitude, and the capacity for working within the frame of an incomplete unfinished world view distinguish [tough-minded] from the more impatient, imaginative, and often aprioristic thinkers in the tender-minded camp." Herbert Feigl, "Logical Empiricism," in *Readings in Philosophical Analysis,* ed. Feigl and Sellars (New York: Appleton-Century-Crofts, 1949), p. 3.

3. John Warwick Montgomery, "The Apologists of Eucatastrophe," in *Myth, Allegory, and Gospel,* ed. John W. Montgomery (Minneapolis: Bethany Publishing House, 1974), p. 26.

4. G. K. Chesterton *(The Ball and the Cross, The Man Who Was Thursday, The Flying Inn)* is spiritual kin to these authors.

5. Anthropologist Claude Levi-Strauss stressed the "astounding similarity between myths collected in widely different regions" of the world while Clyde Kluckhohn and Mircea Eliade found recurrent themes in 50 cultures, including the themes of a "Flood" and a "yearning for Paradise in Primitive traditions" (essentially universal) and a "Slaying of Monsters" theme (found in 37 out of 50 cultures). See Levi-Strauss, "The Structural Study of Myth," *Journal of American Folklore* 68 (1955): pp. 428–45; Kluckhohn, "Recurrent Themes in Myths and Mythmaking," and Mircea Eliade, "The Yearning for Paradise in Primitive Tradition," in *Myth and Mythmaking,* ed. Henry A. Murray (New York: George Braziller, 1960), pp. 51, 61–75. Montgomery concludes as follows: "Does not this "slaying of a monster" have a familiar ring to it (our pun on Tolkien's One Ring is not unintentional!)? Gustaf Aulen has demonstrated the centrality of the *Christus Victor* motif to the entire New Testament message: Jesus, born of a woman, is in fact the Divine Christ who conquers the Evil Power that has brought the race into bondage, and thereby restores mankind. (footnote omitted), From such universal—and therefore impressively Objective—archetypal Motifs can the Christian *litterateur* draw his themes and patterns, thereby creating stories that, if sensitively and artistically executed, are sure to strike to the deep reaches of man's being and point him toward the Christ who fulfilled the myths and legends of the world." Montgomery, "The Apologists of Eucatastrophe," in *Myth, Allegory, and Gospel, p.* 28.

6. C. S. Lewis, *Surprised By Joy* (London: Geoffrey Bles, 1955), p. 222.

7. C. S. Lewis, "Myth Became Fact," in *God in the Dock: Essays on Theology and Ethics,* ed. Walter Hooper (Grand Rapids: Eerdmans, 1970), p. 67. Another fertile area of exploration is the whole genre of detectives in literature who act as Christ figures. One immediately thinks of Chesterton's Father Brown, Dorothy Sayers's Lord Peter Whimsey (Sayers also wrote straight tough-minded apologetical works), and the sine qua non of all great detectives—Arthur Conan Doyle's Sherlock Holmes. Holmes particularly, like Bach, enjoys international and cross-cultural appeal. John Warwick Montgomery's recently released book on Holmes is entitled *The Transcendent Holmes* and argues that Holmes indeed operates as a Christ figure though Conan Doyle himself was a disaster theologically, ending up in the occult and spiritism. In Holmes, we find that "no man spoke as he spoke" and he seems to supernaturally discern the essence of a crime before anyone else. Holmes also sacrifices himself to conquer evil by going over the Reichenbach Falls with his archnemesis, Professor Moriarty. Holmes is then "resurrected" three years later by Conan Doyle and reappears in London. See *The Transcendent Holmes* (Ashcroft, B.C.: Calabash Press, 2000).

8. *Lutheran Worship* 123.

9. The list of Bach scholars who echo this theme is impressive—Karl Geiringer, Gunther Stiller, Albert Schweitzer, Robert L. Marshall, Philipp Spitta, Charles Sanford Terry, Friedrich Blume, and Christoph Wolff. With respect to our point about Bach not composing any operas, Terry points out that the closest Bach came to the genre is found in his secular cantatas (done for various boring civil events such as political appointments). Especially hilarious though is Bach's "Coffee Cantata" (*Schweigt stille, plaudert nicht,* BWV 211), also performed as an operetta, which chronicles a young maiden's addiction to coffee and her devious scheme to write a "coffee exception" into her marriage contract! Terry argues that Bach's use of his daughter's pet name in this cantata suggests he first performed it in his own home. Charles Sanford Terry, *The Music of Bach* (New York: Dover Publications, 1963), p. 102. Terry concludes that the "secular cantatas, on the whole, are less interesting than those he wrote for the church, partly because even his indomitable spirit could not indefinitely suffer the conventional banalities he was invited to clothe with music." Ibid., p. 104.

10. Jaroslav Pelikan, *Bach Among Theologians* (Philadelphia: Fortress Press, 1986), pp. 17–18.

11. Robin A. Leaver, *J. S. Bach as Preacher: His Passions and Music in Worship* (St. Louis: Concordia Publishing House, 1982), p. 13; "Without the vigorous Lutheranism of that time even Johann Sebastian Bach's entire work for the service of worship would not have been possible in its fullness and richness. . . . Wherever Reformed and Pietistic activities became effective in the Lutheran Church, there were disastrous consequences for the practice of church music, as Bach's leaving his Muhlhausen position (a Calvinist court prince) after barely 10 months alarmingly illustrates." Gunther Stiller, *Johann Sebastian Bach and Liturgical Life in Leipzig* (St. Louis: Concordia Publishing House, 1984), pp. 143–44; Charles Sanford Terry,

The Music of Bach (New York: Dover Publications, 1963); See Pelikan, *Bach Among the Theologians,* pp. 42–55 for a discussion of Bach's Lutheran orthodoxy and his commitment musically to the *sola fide* and *sola gratia* of the Reformation. Even Albert Schweitzer, whose *Quest of the Historical Jesus* is hardly a quest for orthodoxy, had to admit that Bach was a thoroughly orthodox Lutheran and "perhaps, the highest among all creative artists." Schweitzer, *J. S. Bach,* 2 vols. (New York: MacMillan & Co., 1958), vol. 1, p. 166.

12. Schweitzer, *J. S. Bach,* vol. 1, p. 30.

13. Robert L. Marshall, *The Music of Johann Sebastian Bach: The Sources, the Style, the Significance* (New York: Simon & Schuster, 1989), p. 68.

14. Terry, *The Music of Bach,* p. 77. As for how Bach accomplished writing more than 300 cantatas (often one per week), see the fascinating account of his weekly schedule while cantor at St. Thomas Church in Leipzig analyzed in depth by both Christoph Wolff and Gunther Stiller. Wolff, *The World of the Bach Cantatas* (New York: W. W. Norton, 1996); Stiller, *Johann Sebastian Bach and Liturgical Life.*

15. Marshall, *Music of Johann Sebastian Bach,* p. 70.

16. Karl Geiringer, *Johann Sebastian Bach: The Culmination of an Era* (New York: Oxford University Press, 1960).

17. Schweitzer, *J. S. Bach,* vol. 1, p. 3

18. One of the most serious modern interpreters of Bach is Maestro Masaki Suzuki, director of the Bach Collegium of Japan.

19. Mendel and David in their work on Bach make plain that Bach, contrary to modern views, was no "stuffed shirt" and certainly not a pietist. His house was full of laughter, coffee, children (he had 20, 9 surviving him), theater, parties, and, of course, music. Bach called wine "a noble gift of God" and cheerfully proclaimed that "I smoke my pipe and worship God." Hans T. David and Arthur Mendel, eds., *The Bach Reader: A Life of Johann Sebastian Bach in Letters and Documents* (New York: W. W. Norton Co., 1945). See pp. 97–98 for one of Bach's poems in honor of the transcendental value of tobacco! We can't resist directing the reader to note the contrast of the Lutheran Bach, whose personal freedom in the Christian life draws directly on Luther, with the rigidity of Calvin, whom Schweitzer says "laughed once." Schweitzer, *J. S. Bach,* vol. 1, p. 20.

20. We also must mention in passing the Christocentric and Scripture-soaked musical efforts of Johannes Brahms, another Lutheran composer strongly in the Reformation tradition. Brahms's *German Requiem* was selected by Maestro Kurt Masur to be played by the New York Philharmonic for the people of New York City at a benefit concert immediately following the tragedy of 9-11.

21. Marshall, *Music of Johann Sebastian Bach,* p. 162.

22. Tom Wolfe, *The Painted Word* (New York: Farrar, Straus & Giroux, 1976), pp. 97–103; see also the excellent discussion of the state of the arts by Gene Edward Veith, where he quotes this passage by Wolfe and then adds: "Wolfe cites Peter Hutchinson's *Arc,* which consisted of a rope with a weight at either end. Attached to the rope were plastic bags filled with gas and rotten vegetables, which

would create more gas as they decayed. This was all thrown into the ocean. The gas bags would lift the rope into an arc. An underwater photographer would come back at regular intervals to record the bursting of the gas bags as the vegetables decayed, the arc collapsed, and the work of art disappeared. The photographs and the 'documentation,' the written account of the idea, were sold to the Museum of Modern Art." Gene Edward Veith, Jr., *The State of the Arts: From Bezalel to Mapplethorpe* (Wheaton: Crossway Books, 1991), p. 93 (citing to Wolfe, *The Painted Word,* p. 104).

23. For an excellent treatment of these issues, see Paul E. Kretzmann, *Christian Art in the Place and in the Form of Lutheran Worship* (St. Louis: Concordia Publishing House, 1921), especially "Choice of Architectural Style," pp. 131 ff. See also Robert E. Wunderlich, *Worship and the Arts* (St. Louis: Concordia Publishing House, 1966), especially pp. 64 ff. addressing church architecture as a "meeting place of all the arts."

24. J. R. R. Tolkien, "On Fairy-Stories," in *Essays Presented to Charles Williams* (London: Oxford University Press, 1947), pp. 83–84.

CHAPTER 10

1. It is fascinating that the harshest, most articulate, and well-reasoned critics of vacuous Evangelical worship styles are Evangelicals or former Evangelicals, or those within orthodox Lutheranism that toyed with Evangelical worship style for a season until they came to their senses. One thinks of *Modern Reformation* magazine (Alliance of Confessing Evangelicals, Philadelphia, PA, Michael S. Horton, editor-in-chief) and *Reformation & Revival* magazine (Reformation and Revival Ministries, Carol Stream, IL, John H. Armstrong, editor-in-chief). For the journey to Rome, see *Evangelical Is Not Enough: Worship of God in Liturgy & Sacrament* by Thomas Howard (San Francisco: Ignatius Press, 1984). Conversion to Eastern Orthodoxy is recorded in Frank Schaeffer's *Dancing Alone: The Quest for Orthodox Faith in the Age of False Religion* (Brookline, MA: Holy Cross Orthodox Press, 1994), and Peter Gillquist's *Becoming Orthodox: A Journey to the Ancient Christian Faith* (Benlomond, CA: Conciliar Press, 1992). The Lutheran point of view is represented by Harold Senkbeil in *Sanctification: Christ in Action* (Milwaukee: Northwestern 1989). Os Guinness has a marvelous book—*Dining with the Devil: The MegaChurch Movement Flirts with Modernity* (Grand Rapids: Baker Books, 1993). Finally, Robert Webber of Wheaton College moved from being a Baptist to being an Episcopalian. Perhaps more than any single person, Webber has been responsible for challenging Evangelicals to discover the liturgical heritage of the Western church. See Robert Webber, *Celebrating Our Faith: Evangelism Through Worship* (San Francisco: Harper & Row, 1986) and *Evangelicals on the Canterbury Trail: Why Evangelicals are Attracted to the Liturgical Church* (Waco: Jarrell, 1985).

2. David Luecke, *Evangelical Style and Lutheran Substance: Facing America's Mission Challenge* (St. Louis: Concordia Publishing House, 1988).

3. See Craig Parton, "Luther Lite and Reformation Schmooze," *Modern Reformation* (January–February 1995: pp. 17–18.

4. *Logia: A Journal of Lutheran Theology*. 15825 373rd Ave., Northville, SD 57465, www.logia.org.

5. A must-read is Walther's theological classic, *The Proper Distinction Between Law and Gospel* (St. Louis: Concordia Publishing House, 1929), which includes such critical distinctions between Law and Gospel as the following: The Law is written on man's heart, while the Gospel can only be known through an act of the Holy Spirit (pp. 7–9); the Law tells us what to do, and the Gospel tells us what God has done (pp. 9, 18–19); the promises of the Law are conditional, while those of the Gospel are without condition (pp. 10–11); the Law contains threats, while the Gospel only announces comfort (p. 11); the Law is for secure sinners, while the Gospel is for terrified sinners (p. 39); every passage of Scripture can be classified as belonging either to the Law or to the Gospel (p. 210); and every sermon must contain both (p. 25). The result for me of reading Walther 10 years before becoming a Lutheran was that I was given a theological roadmap of why I was increasingly miserable living under Evangelical preaching.

6. The Evangelical Lutheran Church of America (ELCA) has about 5 million members, the Lutheran Church—Missouri Synod (LCMS) around 2.6 million, the Wisconsin Evangelical Lutheran Synod (WELS) slightly more than 400,000, and the Evangelical Lutheran Synod (ELS) around 20,000. For a solid and exceedingly fair work on the basic distinctions between Lutherans, Roman Catholics, Eastern Orthodox, and Calvinists or the Reformed, see F. E. Mayer, *The Religious Bodies Of America* (St. Louis: Concordia Publishing House, 1961).

7. Hermann Sasse, *Here We Stand* (Adelaide, South Australia: Lutheran Publishing House, 1979), p. 180. Sasse's book is essential reading for those wishing to delve deeper into the distinction between Lutheranism and the Reformed faith of John Calvin and his followers.

CONCLUSION

1. Mark A. Noll, "The Lutheran Difference," *First Things: A Journal of Religion and Public Life* no. 20 (February 1992): pp. 36–37.

2. J. R. R. Tolkein, *On Fairy Stories: Essays Presented to Charles Williams* (London: Oxford Univer ity Press, 1947), pp. 83–84.